W9-BCV-819

in bip
author not in bip
not in bcl
(3-24-00)

WITHDRAWN
NDSU

# ALLERTON PARK INSTITUTE

## Number 15

*Papers presented at an Institute*
*conducted by the*
*University of Illinois*
*Graduate School of Library Science*
*November 3-6, 1968*

*Allerton Park Institute, 15th, 1968*

# COOPERATION BETWEEN TYPES OF LIBRARIES:

## THE BEGINNINGS OF A STATE PLAN

## FOR

## LIBRARY SERVICES IN ILLINOIS

Edited by

CORA E. THOMASSEN

University of Illinois
Graduate school of Library Science
Urbana, Illinois

223387

© *Copyright 1969*
**by the Board of Trustees of the University of Illinois**
*LC Card Number: 72-625423*

## VOLUMES IN THIS SERIES

*The School Library Supervisor* (Allerton Park Institute No. 1), 1956. $2 paper.

*The Nature and Development of the Library Collection* (No. 3), 1957. $2 paper.

*Collecting Science Literature for General Reading* (No. 7), 1960. $2 paper/$3 cloth.

*The Impact of the Library Services Act: Progress and Potential* (No. 8), 1961. $2 paper.

*Selection and Acquistion Procedures in Medium-Sized and Large Libraries* (No. 9), 1963. $2 paper/$3 cloth.

*The School Library Materials Center: Its Resources and Their Utilization* (No. 10), 1964. $3 cloth.

*University Archives* (No. 11), 1965. $2 paper/$3 cloth.

*The Changing Environment for Library Services in the Metropolitan Area* (No. 12), 1966. $2 paper/$3 cloth.

*Federal Legislation for Libraries* (No. 13), 1967. $2 paper/ $3 cloth.

*Trends in American Publishing* (No. 14), 1968. $4 cloth.

*Cooperation Between Types of Libraries: The Beginnings of a State Plan for Library Services in Illinois* (No. 15), 1969.

# FOREWORD

The Fifteenth Allerton Park Institute sponsored by the faculty of the Graduate School of Library Science of the University of Illinois was conducted from Sunday, November 3 to Wednesday, November 6, 1968, at Allerton Park, the university-owned estate near Monticello, Illinois.

The Institute theme focused on "Cooperation Between Types of Libraries." The conference was supported by the Illinois State Library through funds made available under Title III of the Library Services and Construction Act, as amended in 1966. Illinois librarians representing various types and sizes of libraries were invited to the conference. An attempt was made by the planning committee to have the various regions within the state represented by librarians from the various kinds of libraries located within the several regions. The committee was most interested in creating an environment for interaction among these librarians in order to stimulate greater local cooperative efforts among types of libraries. A related objective was the desire that the beginnings of a state plan for library services in Illinois would emerge.

Speakers of state and national reputation and representing a variety of experiences in different types of libraries were invited to survey past efforts of interlibrary cooperation involving the many facets of library services and to suggest directions in which interlibrary cooperative activities might more effectively be brought into being. The atmosphere of the Institute was one of congenial discussion and interaction among participants and speakers.

The keynote speaker for the conference was Lowell Martin. His paper discusses trends in interlibrary cooperation and traces the history of such efforts nationally, and in Illinois. The kinds of cooperation which have existed among and within types of libraries are discussed, as well as the changing structures of libraries which may lead to greater interlibrary cooperation. Martin projects the possibilities of cooperative efforts through technological innovations which may serve as stimulants to increasing such activities.

Committed to surveying the extent and nature of cooperation between types of libraries in technical service areas, Sarah Vann also directs attention to the ingredients essential to such efforts. Not to be overlooked, Vann maintains, is the element of human resource involvement in cooperative library programs. Vann presents some questions for the self-appraisal of librarians. Librarians' responses to these queries may result in the first steps toward the formulation of a state plan for library services in Illinois.

To determine the extent of interlibrary cooperation among Illinois libraries, Donald Wright conducted a literature search and also used a questionnaire which he submitted to some 500 librarians in the state. The literature search revealed little, but the two hundred and ninety-six respondents to the questionnaire reported some positive experiences as well as some negative attempts at interlibrary cooperation. Wright describes in detail some examples of interlibrary activities which are representative of cooperative efforts within the state.

Drawing from her experience as the Director of School Libraries and Instructional Materials for the state of Hawaii, Carolyn Crawford describes the unique organizational structure affecting library services in that state. The cooperative efforts among public and school libraries in various other states are noted. Crawford admonishes public and school librarians to develop cooperative programs and at the same time to define their separate as well as their mutual responsibilities.

Another paper in this volume is devoted to exploring cooperation between special libraries and other types of libraries. Russell Shank limits his discussion to those special libraries which exist in business, industry, government, museums, societies, and non-profit research agencies. Recognizing the constraints placed on this type of library, Shank goes on to note the relationships that affect special and other types of libraries in systems development. He describes various activities of a cooperative nature but notes that the greatest interaction comes about through "informal or non-systematized contacts." Shank contends that one of the greatest limitations affecting the full utilization of the resources of special libraries is our inability to evaluate collections and then to interfile the subject analyses of the many libraries. Organizing regional agencies must be undertaken—but not before we have sufficient understanding and knowledge of local communities, so as "to find the best configuration of elements to make serviceable systems."

Craig Lovitt, representing the Lieutenant Governor's office in the state of Illinois and assigned to the Office of Intergovernmental Cooperation, describes the work of his office and notes the hierarchy of governmental agencies as they are affected by federal, state, and local governments. He expresses the belief that cooperative action must originate at the local level, that communications must be easy between libraries and other publicly supported organizations, and that recommendations for cooperative efforts should be the joint concern of the professional library associations and state officials and other interested agencies. Lovitt hypothesizes that, "cooperation between people and institutions can contribute much toward creating a community awareness that libraries are essential . . . to our way of life."

Throughout the conference, participants representing different kinds of libraries within a particular region of the state met together in discussion sessions to explore ways in which they might cooperate to provide library services more effectively and efficiently. The edited summaries of those group reports are included at the end of this publication along with the reactions to the reports. A panel of speakers and participants served as reactors. Hopefully the recommendations made by the participants in this conferences *do* represent the beginnings of a state plan for library services in Illinois.

Program planning was directed by Guy Garrison and Herbert Goldhor, Frances B. Jenkins and Cora E. Thomassen of the Graduate School of Library Science faculty. Timothy Sineath, in the Division of University Extension, was responsible for other conference arrangements.

Cora E. Thomassen

# TABLE OF CONTENTS

Lowell A. Martin
*Educational Director,*
*Grolier, Inc., and*
*Director,*
*Chicago Public Library Survey*

# EMERGING TRENDS IN
# INTERLIBRARY COOPERATION

Cooperation among libraries is by no means a fresh and new idea. I need only mention interlibrary loan, centralized cataloging, personal use of reference, bibliographic records of holdings among groups of libraries, and agreements on planned joint acquisition of resources, including one among three large libraries in Chicago that is dated 1895. I do not know when the first book was exchanged between libraries in the United States, but I do know that the February 1913 issue of *Library Journal* carries an article on interlibrary loan that asks how long larger libraries can continue to carry the load of requests from smaller libraries without some compensating return.[1] Illinois began to answer the question half a century later by passing state legislation providing payments to designated reference and research centers.

The early literature does not use the word cooperation as much as we do now, but the term may well apply in its purest meaning to the spontaneous, informal sharing of resources that was fairly common by the turn of the century. For a considerable period, libraries in cities, towns, schools, colleges, and universities were hard pressed to keep up with immediate and mounting local demands, Following this came a considerable lull in concrete cooperative projects among libraries. A man trying to keep his own boat afloat does not have much time to engage in squadron maneuvers with others, but a man who realizes he is destined in time to sink alone, does look around for help.

Librarians began looking around for help in earnest after World War II. The 1944 *Post-War Standards for Public Libraries*[2] incorporated the concept of systems. Research libraries jointly sought to catch up on acquisitions delayed by the war, and finding that they did not come to blows in dividing up accumulated materials, applied the same principle to future acquisitions in the Farmington Plan.

If we apply the word cooperation, in the sense of working together, to the earlier interlibrary activities, then the recent effort might be characterized more as "structured coordination." Actually current plans do not introduce many new kinds of cooperative endeavor or service. What is new are the structures for coordinated action.

This is implied in our dependence on the word "systems." We are seeking to institutionalize cooperation. New York, which has led the way in many respects, now has two congeries of systems: the public library structures and the reference and research agencies, the latter with new boards of directors and new staffs. The bulk of their work to date can be fitted under the same five essentials of planned acquisition, interlibrary loan, interlibrary direct use, comprehensive bibliographic records, and joint technical operations. If the New York reference and research systems had existed fifty years ago, they might have developed much the same programs as are emerging today.

There is a new element, and it might well have a greater impact than structures for coordination. I refer to automation and electronic transmission. Think what facsimile transmission, made practicable and economical, will mean for interlibrary loan as we have known it—we can see the image now rather than getting the book itself two weeks from now. There is a chain effect here: if direct access at a distance can be provided, we must also take a fresh look at planned joint acquisition—it will be more efficient to have a transmission center in one large library than to seek to orchestrate the separate holdings of various libraries. Interesting in this regard is the RAND Corporation report entitled *A Billion Books for Education in America and the World,*[3] with its conjecture about serving specialized America with 100 libraries of 10,000,000 volumes each. Machine-readable bibliographic and cataloging information which will not only affect localized cataloging combines, but will also permit various forms of joint records of holdings must also be considered.

How soon will the mechanized library appear? I would not venture a guess, and it may not come at all in the form now envisioned. I recall that when I shifted to publishing ten years ago and found myself caught up in endless publishers' luncheons, one could bring down the group at the table in derisive glee by telling the newest story on how the computer had loused up a recent publishing venture. Today practically every one of these publishers works with machine-readable tape for setting type, justifying margins, hyphenating words, laying out pages, and assigning page numbers.

Publishers' luncheon tables are not amused by computer stories today. They have returned to talking as publishers, about what books are needed and how they can be created. The automated library will no more eliminate librarians than automated printing has eliminated publishers. It will simply permit them to concentrate on practicing librarianship, which has to do with what resources people need and how to provide them.

## LIBRARY COOPERATION TODAY

In the last decade or two, some librarians have moved beyond mere talk about cooperation to genuine concern about the limitations of their own resources; efforts and growing interest in what might be accomplished jointly are prevalent. This is an intangible move, occuring in the minds of library officials, but it is a first requirement if service is to get off dead center. Where this psychic step has not been taken, and there are many places where it has not, precisely there is where joint action among libraries is absent or lagging.

I believe that concern exists to a degree on the part of the serveral types of librarians—public, academic, school, and special. Up to this point we are dealing with an outlook that is not confined to one or another type of library.

The second step of contact and consultation has taken place in many localities, states and regions. The plant of cooperation grows under the glow of direct human exchange. It is a source of comfort to find that others are in the same fix as you are, and is further reassuring to hear that by holding hands members of a group may more effectively meet their common problems. Meetings at this stage are likely to have considerable warmth but few tangible results.

It is here at the early stage of contact and consultation that the libraries of the several types part company. Each group has its own problems and hopes, separate from those of other types of libraries. Small wonder that in the succeeding steps—making plans, getting money, establishing structures of cooperation—the types of libraries have for the most part gone their own ways.

The concerned and consulting group is likely to make plans, big or small. That stage is marked here in Illinois by the Rohlf Report,[4] and I suspect that one could find less formal plans among groups of college and school libraries in the state. It follows from the parting of the ways at the preceding step of consultation that most such plans are for one type of library.

The fanciest plans have been for public libraries. The published standards for this kind of library assume joint endeavor. Federal funds have been used for cooperative public library planning. The state library agencies—which for the most part are really public library agencies—have either sponsored planning or engaged in it themselves.

To this point librarians have been mostly talking to each other. Now with a plan in hand they must talk to the holders of the purse strings. The reason why money has been essential is that the plans really do not propose cooperation among libraries. What they propose is new agencies in one form or another—usually called systems—to which libraries can go to get the advantages of a larger unit. I think the distinction is more than semantic or technical, as we will see shortly in analyzing existing public library systems.

The response from government sources of money has been encouraging. Illinois librarians have found that it is possible to present the cause of libraries to state officials and get a positive response. Other states have also had a degree of success, even when their plans were not made as carefully as those of Illinois. If nothing else could be claimed for the cooperative systems concept, it has proven to be a means to focus attention on library needs and to open added channels of support. If you are inclined to be cynical, you might push this a step further and wonder whether these systems programs in some states were really designed to promote cooperation or to tap state money.

My theme at the moment is that there has been a discernible advance through the several steps of the cooperative sequence among libraries. We are in a mood for joint action.

## PUBLIC LIBRARY SYSTEMS

While public library systems are by no means the only form of current library cooperation, they are at present the most active spot and preempt much of our attention. They deserve review here both as a trend in themselves and as an indication of the direction in which we are moving. While they do not formally involve various types of libraries, we may be able to learn from them.

The cooperative library system is the modern version of the larger unit library. The earlier form was the county or multi-county library, to which we gave a generation of effort, only to realize after building a thousand county libraries that this was really not what was meant by modern library service. We had to learn the hard way that the combination of weak agencies into a unit serving a larger piece of territory did not make for effective service. It took twenty-five years to learn this lesson. The experience should make us less than confident that we have since found revealed truth.

Now, rather than building up county or multi-county libraries, the approach is through the system—meaning by this a coordinating structure of some kind, retention of local autonomy, voluntary participation, flexibility of territory, and selectivity of projects. The individual library needs to do very little to become a member of a system, and must continue to partake of very little in order to remain in the fold. The present-day library system is most permissive. This is at once its strength and its weakness.

A rich variety of state plans have grown up within this framework. New York broke though by creating separate library centers within regions, around which individual libraries could gather to share resources and services provided for them. Pennsylvania is betting its money on existing larger libraries spread throughout the state, thus avoiding an added bureaucracy. California does not have a uniform state-wide pattern but sponsors decentralized cooperative ventures, with the result that the North Bay group is quite different from the Black Gold cooperative centered on Santa Barbara, and this in turn is different from the regional reference program based in Fresno. Maryland starts from its foundation of county libraries covering the state and instead of multi-purpose cooperative units adds interlibrary agencies for distinct functions—new processing centers, interlibrary loan and, shortly, interlibrary reference centered on the Enoch Pratt Free Library in Baltimore. The variety among state plans for library systems is one of the most encouraging signs in the picture.

The Illinois plan has elements of several of these, and it remains to be seen whether it is the best eclectic combination for the circumstances. The systems design is taken from the New York model and the reference and research design from Pennsylvania. Given these sources, I would like to make an obvious suggestion; New York has just completed one of the very few evaluations we have of systems programs in any depth.[5] The prime effort in that evaluation was not to analyze structure as such, but to assess its effect on service, down in the local library. In over-simplified summary, in many smaller libraries there were discernibly more books available to the reader, in some libraries use of interlibrary loan doubled, and in a few libraries there was demonstrable improvement in staff service in the form of reference and advisory performance. You may have noted that progression of terms from *many* for better resources, to *some* for opening a wider world through interlibrary loan, to a *few* for effect on staff performance. The toughest job in a systems program is to improve service in the front lines, the quality of performance of staff in local libraries. Note also in the New York evaluation report the mounting strain that was found on the systems structures at the point of the central or headquarters libraries. You will also find in that report a reaching for a regional base for both service and financial purposes that is larger than the natural contiguous local systems.

As to the Pennsylvania reference and research program, there has been no detailed evaluation of this except in the recent re-survey in that state[6], but you will find benefit in going through the minutes of meetings and noting the program developed by the council of the four regional resource libraries.

Let me now return to a closer look at common elements and possible problems in public library systems as they have developed. Their most frequent services are interlibrary loan, building up of reserve resources, and advice and consultation for local staff. Does this have a familiar ring? Of course—it is the standard program of state library agencies, as set forth in considerable variety in the 1963 *Standards for Library Functions at the State Level.*[7] Rather than being billed as cooperation in the sense of several units sharing strength and each helping the other, the usual library system might better be described as a localized state library service agency, financed by state funds, providing various services of particular value to smaller libraries, and used by local units alert enough to take advantage of them.

This characterization is not intended to diminish systems but to place them within the spectrum of library cooperation. I am disturbed when existing local systems are somehow assumed to be the sum and apex of interlibrary cooperation; they are, on the contrary, only a start, and indeed are simply a more localized way of doing what we have done in the past.

Seen in this light, we can more objectively consider questions about these new systems. They call for relatively little commitment on the part of local libraries. Library systems only slowly develop a sense of widespread identification that would hold them together in time of stress. Until then they are more like dispensers of aid to underdeveloped countries, and those who receive are not always as grateful as the giver would wish. The first test comes two or three years after systems are formed, when promise has become reality, and some libraries feel disappointed. Another test comes when the largest and strongest units in the enterprise assess what they get out of the system program as compared with what they could get on their own with their share of the system funds. We are dealing with a tenuous structure, held together not so much by mutual benefit and common sacrifice as by persuasion, gifts and a call to remote professional standards. Under the circumstances the systems directors would do well not to be too concerned about job security.

I would like to see more required of local libraries for participation in cooperative ventures. The sustaining power of a joint project that I enter with you is that we each put something in, thus feeling that the enterprise is our own, and we each get something out, thus feeling that it is worth the effort. I cannot rightly call this an emerging trend because system directors, like their forebears in the state capitol, tend to hold up the prospect of rich rewards for little sacrifice, and hesitate to mobilize a genuine mutual aid society where each member has to contribute. One hard contribution could be in the form of money to support expanded system programs decided upon jointly by the members themselves, the money not to be deducted from already limited local funds, but coming perhaps from the county level which also has an inter-jurisdictional library interest, or from new region-wide library districts.

Some localities do not participate in systems programs right from the beginning. Others—a larger number—are technically part of the system but participate as little as professional and public opinion will allow. Do not make the mistake of equating the theoretical opportunity for system benefits with the actuality of better service for all the people. Many Americans are getting better library service through agencies participating in organized cooperative programs in their areas, but many more—in and out of the system, not holdouts and dropouts alone—are exactly where they were before. I anticipate increasing concern about the non-participants, more direct pressure through granting or withholding of state funds to get them in, and in time clearer state criteria and regulations defining participation.

Most of the public library ststems exist as the result of a transfusion of state money. Interestingly this is not the case in California, which is far behind others in state aid to libraries. Yet in some areas of that state there is more local action in interlibrary cooperation than in some of the states making substantial grants. California lacks state funds but has local commitment. I am uneasy about other states that have money from the state capital but minimum local interest and concern. I hope this type of involvement is not one of the emerging trends in joint library organization. Passing the buck, shifting the problem to the systems area or region or state, getting outside money, setting up a separate center so that we can each go back to our own office and let someone else worry about interlibrary development would be disastrous for library cooperation. From this little excursion into public library systems, we can extract some fairly tangible trends that are likely to appear also in cooperation among types of libraries: building of new structures, assignment of separate personnel to the job, infusion of fresh funds from the outside, dependence on voluntary participation, flexibility in both the territorial and the governmental bases, and a search for equity to compensate larger libraries which give more than they receive in joint action.

## ARE WE PREPARING FOR 1970 OR 1950?

For all the present activity, library systems have been slow to get moving. The concept in its present form is at least twenty-five years old. The same comment of slow development applies to other forms of cooperation, whether within or among types of libraries.

This could be dismissed as the subjective judgment of an impatient man, except that it leads to a further and more disturbing question. Our present modes of cooperation were conceived a generation ago. They were designed to meet the needs of the immediate postwar world. Now twenty years later we are just beginning to move on a wide scale. Could it be that using the concepts of the past we will get library service suitable only for the past? I am trying to say that a well-developed library service in the present systems pattern might have been equal to the demands of 1950 but may not be equal to 1970.

Why equal to 1950 but not to 1970? What really has changed in the interval? This is not the place to go into a detailed statement of the trends of the times, but let me simply remind you of a few factors that have profoundly changed in twenty years and which will almost surely continue to do so in the next two decades. As a society we came out of the depression and the war with the narrow purpose of getting our economic system back to normal productivity. What it took us longer to see was that in the process the very nature of that system had changed, from a base of energy to a base of knowledge. In making stock market investments today, for example, it is wise not to select the company with the greatest productivity but the firm with the most active research program and the greatest reservoir of human brainpower. It is no accident that we have many more students and that their numbers are increasing most rapidly at the higher levels of education.

One could pick up various social trends and develop them in many directions to show the likely differences between library requirements twenty years hence and twenty years in the past. Let me develop just one trend, growing out of my reference to a society of specialists. (By specialists I refer not solely to researchers within universities and laboratories but to individuals throughout our society who work, read and get information within defined and particularized areas.) My point is that each of these individuals function less in a limited spatial community and more in a far-flung special-interest community. Of course they operate locally as parent or grocery shopper or church goer. But in their specialties, for which they seek library resources, they are part of a wide fraternity and communication network, and they have more contacts, read about and exchange ideas more extensively within this far-flung network than they do with the neighbor three doors away.

Yet the public library, for one, is a space-oriented institution, a delivery system defined by territory. It is for this city, that town, the other county. It has branches in local neighborhoods. The concept behind it is how far a person will go to get a physical book. If he will not go beyond the crossroads, we will send a bookmobile there. But if we take the increasing number of individuals who are also specialists as our users, and bring in emerging communication devices as means to get resources to them, we have a new ball game.

The question shifts from how far the user will go to get the book, to how far we will shortly be able to send the book to him. Instead of asking how many blocks or floors the reader will walk or how many miles he will drive his car, we might better ask what is the practical working radius of Telestar. We are an earth-boud institution. As and if spatial limitations are removed, the implications for the structure of library service are profound, and also the implications for relating ourselves directly and selectively to the motives of readers. This leads me to one trend that I sincerely hope emerges—the building of evaluation into any cooperative library endeavor. Illinois is spending substantial sums to improve interlibrary loan. But is information on who is using this service, for what purpose, with what results, at what speed, and at what cost being gathered? Interlibrary cooperation will be a winding path of disillusionment unless we stand off and judge ourselves as we go along.

The recent national study of public library systems by the Nelson Associates organization was an attempt to evaluate an important cooperative trend, but it fell short of its mark. To begin with, they had $50,000 to judge 1,000 agencies, which works out to $50 a shot. Even then, significant returns might have been achieved if libraries had adequate before-and-after data on what they are doing, but this was not the case. I advise that Illinois should not venture too far on a systems program, or on any other cooperative venture, before taking stock.

## COOPERATION AMONG TYPES OF LIBRARIES

Shifting the base of cooperative planning to the various types of libraries might provide a means not only to get more riders on the present bandwagon but also to jointly plan new vehicles. This starts with the very framework within which we think about the totality of library service. Our taxonomy has an institutional base. We speak of the four kinds of libraries—actually they could be grouped into three kinds, or five, or more—which are defined by the type of organization that foots the bill: government, school, university or business-industry. Thus, when we refer to cooperation among types of libraries, we mean in part not solely cooperation among libraries but between this city and that school and the college at the edge of town and the large industry out in the industrial park. We have not only the separateness of libraries to bridge but also the separateness of these discrete parts of our governmental-educational-economic fabric. It is one thing to get the several libraries to agree, but another to get the city council and the board of education and the trustees of the university and the manager of the aerospace company to sign a contractual agreement. But by accomplishing this, libraries may find that their programs get much more attention from officials.

In the process of achieving cooperation planners may have to re-think their roles and functions. For example, we very much need an agreed upon division of responsibilities between public and school libraries. But this in turn rests upon clarification of just what the school conceives to be 1) its proper scope and limits and 2) its achievable performance in providing the resources needed by its students, and equally upon clarification of 1) just what part the public library should properly play and 2) how far it can responsibly commit itself in the light of its other publics and objectives. These turn out to be soul-wrenching questions; and, once again the relevant data are often lacking. I find that when discussion starts between school and public librarians, there is no clear evidence of just what high-school students need or actually seek, or even of what teachers ask them to seek; ask teachers and you get one answer, ask librarians and you get another. In a research project now getting underway in Philadelphia we are going directly to students themselves for the answer.

In the process of planning across the lines separating types of libraries, we will need to drop our institutional provincialism and think more in terms of library users and library functions. There is more than one way to cut the library pie—it does not necessarily have to be quartered into the four existing kinds of libraries.

One alternative approach is in terms of groups of users. There are children, students, the individuals as specialists I have mentioned, and other groups, and each seeks different materials and uses them in a different way. It is interesting that when one mentally starts from scratch and imagines the proper and ideal facilities for each of these groups, that the results vary widely for each. Yet as most libraries are now organized we often combine facilities for several types in one agency. This is particularly true of the public library but it also applies elsewhere in the prevailing structure; for example, every university librarian is conscious of the push and pull between provision for students and provision for researchers. There are also very different library needs required for the people in the city ghetto and for the people in the remodeled brownstones and in the high-rise apartments not far away. The former presents a challenge that is raising questions as to the very role of the public library. The latter constitute our most cosmopolitan public, those who conceivably may be an inner force that can help rebuild the city. Rather than a more-or-less standard branch seeking to serve both and not right for either, and a more or less standard school library, serving both, planners could consider the possibilities of a new kind of group library for each, which could serve the total range of needs and interests of its own public, students and adults alike.

Another alternative is by function to be served. Let your imagination go on a library specifically designed to provide information—England and France have both gone in this direction—or to meet the growing cultural interest (the library cultural center) or the mounting concern with technological development (the library technological center).

I, of course, am not advocating that we tear down our public and school and university and other libraries and build new agencies explicitly for children or students or researchers or information seekers or culture vultures, but I do think it is a growing concern for meeting better the needs of the various groups that pushes us toward cooperation among types of libraries. The same individuals come into your institution as into mine, and we find when we sit down that they are coming to both of us for the same purpose, and we may even go further and admit that neither of us is doing very well by them. Here is the beginning of wisdom. We may be stuck with the institutional division into types of libraries, but we have an opportunity to develop joint programs to overcome some of the disadvantages of this arrangement, seeking out the groups of readers and the functions of reading now not well served.

Another emerging trend, which may well be abetted by planning between types of libraries, is to take a fresh look at the geography or territorial base of library cooperation. How large should a cooperating group of libraries be—the school and public library within a small town, the libraries within an existing system, all the libraries in a large region or whole state, or even beyond the state boundaries? There is of course no one answer. One kind of program may be built on how far librarians can conveniently go to meet periodically, another on how far the user will go to get resources, another on how far one can make a telephone call without paying a toll, on up to the distance and cost factors in rapid electronic transmission.

We should beware of accepting without question the geographic limits of any existing cooperative programs. It could be that the recently-created public library systems in Illinois are transitional structures, to be replaced in time by more appropriate units. As the systems mature, and their directors have time to look ahead, they will be thinking of inter-system possibilities—maybe inter-system necessities. One such necessity could be a far broader tax base, the comprehensive library district, larger than present conceptions, because a good system is not going to rest with what it can accomplish with forty cents per capita, or fifty cents or even one dollar.

Special geographical factors enter into the picture in metropolitan areas and along state boundaries. I doubt whether wholesale annexation of smaller places will occur on any wide scale around big cities, but I do anticipate new special-purpose functional agencies to deal with matters that cut across arbitrary governmental lines. This need has been easiest to see in matters of transportation and water supply and sanitation. It has been less clear in education, and as a result some of the best and some of the worst schooling in the country is available within metropolitan centers. Libraries have started to cross these lines. In some form I anticipate the metropolitan library agency, perhaps growing from the present systems—certainly I hope that the one step of systems will not be interpreted as perfection and prevent further needed structural development. Or the process of enlargement may take the form of systems for systems, for special purposes, such as automated cataloging, or a bibliographical communication center, or an information bank.

State boundaries are a parallel problem. I have yet to be involved in a state-wide study that did not to some extent involve adjacent states. In Pennsylvania there is a whole northern tier that is oriented to cities above the New York border, in New Jersey one of the severe problem areas is directly across the Delaware River from Philadephia. Even in California, people living east of the Sierra Nevada go much more frequently to Reno than they do over the mountains to Sacramento.

Larger structures, greater territories, the far-flung interest group—but what about decentralization and local control? This applies to libraries as well as to schools. We may fortunately have the ingredients to keep the scales in balance in our field. The individual local library on the one side, the interlibrary cooperative structure on the other. As you build higher, do not neglect the foundation. Indeed, the purpose in the end is not a fancy super-structure but greater strength where resources and people meet.

## References

1. Hicks, Frederick C. "Inter-Library Loans," *Library Journal,* 38:72, Feb. 1913.

2. American Library Association. *Post-War Standards for Public Libraries.* Chicago, ALA Committee on Post-War Planning, 1943.

3. Hays, David G. *A Billion Books for Education in America and the World.* Santa Monica, Calif., The Rand Corporation, 1968.

4. Rohlf, Robert H. *A Plan for Public Library Development in Illinois.* Aurora, Ill., Illinois Library Association, 1963.

5. New York (State) Division of Evaluation. *Emerging Library Systems; the 1963-66 Evaluation of the New York State Library Systems.* Albany, University of the State of New York, 1967.

6. Martin, Lowell A., *et al. Progress and Problems of Pennsylvania Libraries; a Re-Survey.* Harrisburg, Pennsylvania State Library, 1967.

7. American Assocation of State Librarians. *Standards for Library Functions at the State Level.* Chicago, ALA, 1963.

Sarah K. Vann
*Professor, School of Information and*
*Library Studies*
*State University of New York*
*at Buffalo*

# COOPERATION BETWEEN DIFFERENT TYPES OF LIBRARIES IN TECHNICAL SERVICES

The potency of the melding of the terms *cooperation, between types of libraries,* and *technical services* requires some awareness of the ingredients before a comment can be made concerning the effect of such a melding. It seems appropriate, therefore, first to formulate some definitions, and then to survey statewide centralized processing services and state library involvement—in action and as anticipated through some of the recommendations and plans being made.

## Definition of Terms

Cooperation in technical services has tended to be identified with centralized processing which is essentially a coined phrase combining two quite distinct concepts, processing and centralization, the latter of which is generally dependent on cooperation. The words to be defined are: processing, centralization, cooperation, and human resource involvement.

*Processing* designates services relating to acquisition and analyses of resources and the recording of data for the use of a library's public. It may encompass one or more of the following phases of service: a) selection (in an advisory or almost compulsory plan); b) acquisition/ordering (of all or certain kinds of materials); c) analyses of content, descriptive and subject (whatever the format); d) recording of data (whatever the technology employed); and e) finishing details (pocketing, pasting, etc.).

When processing services are limited to analyses of content, descriptive and subject, and the recording of and dispersal of appropriate data, a more precise definition is information flow or information data services.

*Centralization* implies unification of variants of some kind for the anticipated achievement of a common goal—and in the present definition—a goal of processing centrally within the limitations of one or more of the phases of services earlier identified.

The recipients of such processing services may include one or more types of libraries such as public, school, academic, special, and/or information centers and/or also may be:

a) Part of one autonomous library and its array of branches, units, special departments, etc.

b) One of a cluster of autonomous libraries of uni- or multi- type which share a common product.

c) A library within a system/district/county/regional structuring of public libraries as in California, New York, and Pennsylvania.

d) A library, local or regional, wherein the state has assumed a responsibility for technical services as in Georgia and Hawaii.

e) A library in one state reaching across state boundaries and barriers to participate in a centralized processing program in another state, as in Delaware.

*Cooperation,* according to *The Random House Dictionary,* is defined as:

"1. an act or instance of working together for a common purpose or benefit; joint action. 2. more or less active assistance from a person, association, etc. . . . . 3. willingness to cooperate."[1]

Also it is inevitable, because of its elusiveness, that personalized definitions will continue to be given for cooperation. With less ambiguity than that illustrated in the dictionary, an experienced director of more than one centralized processing program has offered the following view: "I have found that the word 'cooperation' is one with which all librarians profess to agree, but to which, in reality, they render only 'lip service.' Cooperation is fine for the other fellow but 'in my library it just can't be done that way.' "

Equally difficult to define is the spirit of cooperation with which the search for and acceptance of centralization are imbued—both the responsibility assumed by an agency offering centralized services and the responsibility accepted by the recipient of the services. This may be called the human resource aspect in contrast to the technical resource aspect. It is, in the end, far more pervasive, far more deterministic than any other factor involved, however sophisticated the technology.

The human resource involvement in centralized processing and response to that involvement have been reported in a 1967 study of the view of seventy-five member/recipient libraries.[2] Of the total, sixty-two or 82.7 percent, indicated that upon joining the center with which each was associated, each had agreed to accept the centralized services as defined in agreements, manuals, and the like, prepared by the center. In twelve instances the agreement had been principle only while one indicated that no agreement had been made.

Yet, of the sixty-two libraries, thirty-seven, or 60 percent, reported that they accepted the data on catalog cards without change. The multiplicity of reasons given for the necessity for making changes were divided into those relating to local adaptations and to criticisms of cataloging by centers. With such evidence, it seems timely to inquire if there has not been a bit of self-delusion in identifying a library's association with a processing center as truly cooperative.

## SURVEY OF STATEWIDE CENTRALIZED PROCESSING
## SERVICES AND STATE LIBRARY INVOLVEMENT

### Centralized Processing Services in States

Because of the need for the latest information on activities within states, a letter was sent in the summer of 1968 to forty-nine of the fifty state libraries. The fiftieth state, Illinois, was represented at this Institute by Margaret Shreve, administrator of the Book Processing Center, Oak Park, who offered some pentrating and practical observations. The extraordinary response to the inquiry by forty-two of the states, or 87 percent, implies a nationwide interest in the program of this Institute and in the decisions yet to be made by the librarians of Illinois.

*The Profile.* The profile of centralized activities within the technical services area is limited to thirty-four states since eight indicated that they offered no centralized processing services. The centralized activities of the thirty-four states are as follows:

| *Centralized activities* | *Number of states* |
|---|---|
| Centralized processing services for: | |
| College libraries only | 1 |
| School libraries only | 2 |
| Public libraries only | 12 |
| Regional libraries only | 3 |
| Centralized processing services for more than one type of library | 16 |
| Total | 34 |

The profile, if further delineated, would reveal variations among the centralized processing programs. For such information, Illinois librarians are invited to make a thorough and critical study of the data included in the *Southeastern Pennsylvania Processing Center Feasibility Study,* published by the Pennsylvania State Library in 1967.[3] It is an appraisal, accurate as of 1966, of the then known existing programs and/or centers and includes data relating to characteristics such as: 1) legal and financial, 2) internal organization and activity, 3) membership, 4) physical environment, and 5) internal activities within a center.

### Multi-type Library Membership

The sixteen states which noted in their responses that centralized processing centers in their states have multi-type library membership can be identified readily but without comment on the extent or quality of the services as follows: California, Georgia, Hawaii, Idaho, Kentucky, Minnesota, Mississippi, Nevada, New York, North Carolina, North Dakota, Ohio, Pennsylvania, Washington, West Virginia, and Wyoming.

This represents a significant increase when compared to the four which included public and school libraries in their membership in 1965. In that year the Missouri State Library made a "Survey of Processing Centers" to which twenty-five centers responded. Of that number, thirteen centers identified their membership as public library only while four, as earlier stated, included public and school libraries.[4] Membership in the twenty-three centers as of the date of the Missouri survey follow:

| *Type of library membership* | *Number of centers (as of 1965)* |
|---|---|
| Public (including city, county, and regional) | 13 |
| Public and school | 4 |
| Public and state agencies | 2 |
| Public and college/university | 2 |
| Public, school, and academic | 1 |
| Public and some institutions | 1 |
| Total | 23 |

Thus, while the majority of those responding included only one type, the reality of multi-type library involvement is evident. The responses support the view of Mary Lee Bundy's 1962 study on *Public Library Processing Centers: a Report of a Nationwide Survey* wherein fourteen centers "commented on the desirability of keeping membership limited to similar types of libraries."[5]

Among centers which have included public and school libraries as recipients of their services are: the Pinal County Free Library of Arizona, the State Catalog Service of Georgia, the State Library of Hawaii, the Wayne County Library System of Michigan, and the Library Services Center of Eastern Ohio.

There has been some objection to such an extension of service, for example, one member library expressed resentment to "non-member" participation by school libraries because:

non-member schools receive custom cataloging—in that their children's books are cataloged more according to Wilson headings and numbers . . . . I believe that members' orders should take precedence over non-members.[6]

Although a few college libraries have contracted for processing services, they have for the most part thus far expressed little enthusiasm for such projects. Examples of college libraries which are or have been participants may be found in Ohio, where the State Library reported that its processing services had been extended to the Dayton Branch of the Ohio State University and Miami University; in California, where the Monterey Peninsula College Library participates in the Monterey County Library program and, as of 1968, the Black Gold Cooperative Library System of Ventura which welcomed one college library; and in New York, where the Nioga Library System contracted with two local academic institutions and found itself compelled to implement policies which differed from those for its public library membership. As of 1968 the future of the Nioga relationship was reported as uncertain.

Of the centers which include multi-type library membership, two, Georgia and Hawaii, represent statewide programs. Brief extracts from their recent annual reports suggest the contributions each is making. In Georgia, the scope of services, while not so identified, is information flow in that catalog data—sets of catalog cards only—have been furnished for library books purchased through the State Department of Education if the titles are requested on current purchase orders from school or public libraries. In the annual report of 1967/68 of the *Georgia State Catalog Service,* the statewide service was

| *Distribution by type of library* | *Number of sets of catalog cards distributed, 1967/68* |
|---|---|
| To public libraries | 71,292 |
| To school libraries | 298,131 |
| Total sets distributed | 369,423 |

Of the total sets distributed, 6,432 were for titles cataloged during the year of the report.[7]

In Hawaii, the Hawaii State Library, under the direction of James R. Hunt, formerly of the Wayne County Library System, has introduced a statewide program which includes all the book requests from forty-five public libraries and about 250 school libraries. In the annual report for 1966/67, the Centralized Processing Center reported that 49,132 titles were processed for the two types of libraries with the following distribution:

| *Type of library* | *New titles processed* | *Added titles processed* |
|---|---|---|
| Public | 11,186 | 15,658 |
| School | 5,372 | 16,916 |

Both musical scores and phonorecords were included as new and added titles. Because of duplication of titles acquired by both types of libraries, the total of new and added titles was actually 34,059. Of that total, 9,338 were identified as new adult and juvenile titles.[8]

The State Librarian has made the following evaluation of his program:

> We believe our Centralized Processing Center is the largest in the country. We also believe that we are the most efficient. . . . We do anticipate that for the current fiscal year the Centralized Processing Center will handle over 400,000 volumes. We had hoped to reach that figure last year, however, we had many setbacks—the most critical being a flooding of the entire Center which destroyed approximately $85,000 worth of material. Therefore, our production only reached 318,000 volumes.[9]

### State Library Involvement

While the profile as sketched has noted the multi-type library membership of two state programs, little reference has been made to the rapid involvement of state libraries with centralized processing programs. Yet, so extensive is its participation, that the time is seemingly near for the inevitable demise of the autonomously structured or the neo-departmentally structured center unless such a program can become a part of a statewide systems program being financed in part or in whole by state and federal funds. While state libraries have not sought the responsibility—indeed many have had such "greatness" thrust upon them—the position of strength has resulted from the routing of federal monies for library services through state libraries.

The *Southeastern Pennsylvania Processing Center Feasibility Study* noted that the range of participation of state libraries in centralized processing extended, "From the nothingness of some states to the recently launched ambitious program of the Texas State Library which as of July 1, 1965, inaugurated an automatic data processing program as a pilot project of the State Library under the Libraries Services and Construction Act."[10] Brief references to the activities of fourteen additional state libraries—in the states of California, Florida, Georgia, Hawaii, Idaho, Kentucky, Michigan, Nevada, New Hampshire, New York, North Carolina, Ohio, Oklahoma, and Wyoming—are made in the *Study*. Of these, only the State Library of Idaho reported the dissolution, as of 1965, of its centralized book processing because the service, according to the state plan, would be dispersed among the proposed six regional library systems.[11]

Such assignment to the proposed system libraries was, at the time, imitative of the existing systems program in New York State. Even at that time, however, New York State was seeking a solution to the excessive fragmentation of duplicative processing activities among its systems by the possible creation of one cataloging and acquisition center for all its public libraries.

Though the Texas State Library soon after the completion of the *Study* phased out its centralized processing center, the observation in the *Study* that "the State Library towers currently . . . as a centrifugal force in coordinating a processing program" continues to characterize statewide planning. That some concern about the future was being expressed can be found in the slightly prescient warning that accompanied that observation: "Even as State Libraries assume more active roles, one State Library staff member has cautioned about and questioned the wisdom of centering the program in a State Library because of the political structure and budgetary pressures which generally affect processing before [it affects] public service functions."[12] As of 1968 similar warning signals have emanated from two additional states wherein the state library has been offering some form of centralized processing services.

That state libraries have become involved has thus been demonstarted. Of historical importance may be the factors which have invited or compelled such action and, of current import, whither the multi-type library membership commitment.

### Origins of State Library Involvement

Originally centralized and widely varied processing centers and/or programs emerged as valiant, determined efforts to achieve what has been called a "calculated interdependence."[13] In many of these, survival was made possible by the timely assistance of the federal government which routed monies through an intermediary—the state library—rather than directly to the indigent.

Activated by such pressures and incentives as instant affluence, broadened but ill-defined responsibilities for planning, and by personnel crises, state librarians requested the Library Services Branch of the U.S. Office of Education to sponsor a conference on statewide planning. Such a conference was held in 1965, the papers and discussion of which may be found in *Statewide Long-Range Planning for Libraries.*[14]

An obvious corollary to the concept of statewide planning is the extension of that planning to all types of libraries. This would be particularly reflected in planning, which is always futuristic in contrast to implementing, which is always present, and sometimes perfect, although occasionally imperfect. Thus, in Lowell Martin's paper on "Principles of Statewide Planning," the librarian advised that "A statewide library plan by definition and by necessity should look forward to an interrelated program among all types of libraries."[15] Such an omni-principle might have sounded somewhat ominous had the word cooperative been used rather than interrelated, though the latter clearly implies a reciprocal relationship. While it has been shown earlier that some centralized processing centers/programs had extended their services to more than one type of library, the reasons for so doing had rarely been accompanied, other than at the state library level, by meditations on statewide responsibilities, interrelated programs among the types of libraries, or, indeed, on cooperative goals. Nevertheless, whether recent emphasis on statewide planning has been a casual or a concomitant factor, recommendations are being made for statewide centralization of aspects of technical services for multi-type library membership.

### Statewide Recommendations

The contents of *Statewide Library Surveys and Development Plans: An Annotated Bibliography, 1956-1967*[16] attest to the continuing search by state libraries and other agencies for solutions to the problems inherent in statewide planning. The bibliography was designed purposefully for the following two reasons: (1) to indicate the present status of statewide library planning, and (2) to serve as a guide for those who are involved in statewide planning or who might wish to see examples of what has been done.[17]

While the studies vary in scope, perception, and recommendations, the commonality both of the problems identified and of the surveyors used is readily apparent. There is at least one study cited for forty-four of the fifty states and for New York State, twenty-eight studies are cited. The six states not represented are Alabama, Alaska, Florida, Minnesota, Mississippi, and New Mexico. Since the bibliography was compiled, a study on *Centralized Processing for the State of Florida*[18] has appeared. Therefore, as of November 1968, only five of the fifty states had not made available their recommendations, if any, for statewide development.

The availability of the comprehensive, annotated bibliography on *Statewide Library Surveys and Development Plans* eliminated the need for adding to this paper an inventory of the studies pertaining specifically to centralized processing. Instead, recommendations as found in officially sponsored studies are to be used as illustrative of the current syndrome. The recommendations, with additional data and observations, have been extracted from studies made for the states of New York, Pennsylvania, Louisiana, Massachusetts, and Florida, all of which were published between 1966 and 1968.

*Recommendations for New York State.* Studies for New York State, the first major ones to be published following the 1965 conference on statewide, long-range planning, were made by Nelson Associates, Inc., in 1966, when that firm was presumably at its apogee of influence within the state. Among the many Nelson studies are the following three concerned specifically with technical services: *Feasibility of School and College Library Processing Through Library Systems in New York State; The Feasibility of Further Centralizing the Technical Processing Operations of the Public Libraries of New York City;* and *Centralized Processing for the Public Libraries of New York State.*

While there was an original hypothesis concerning multi-type library involvement in a common centralized processing program, the findings of the *Feasibility of School and College Library Processing* were less than supportive of such an hypothesis or of the encompassing recommendation finally made in *Centralized Processing for Public Libraries* for the creation of one center. The findings and/or recommendations of the three studies are listed below:

1) In the *Feasibility of School and College Library Processing,* of the forty-three systems expressing a preference as to type of processing facility, thirty-three, or 77 percent, chose one which would serve school libraries alone. Forty-seven public school systems responded to the question concerning an advantage in centralization on a statewide basis as follows:

| *Response*[19] | *Public School Systems Responding* | |
|---|---|---|
| | Number | Percent |
| Saw an advantage in centralization of acquisition and processing on a statewide basis | 34 | 72% |
| Saw no advantage | 12 | 26% |
| Said any advantage would depend on the way in which such an operation was organized | 1 | 2% |

Similarly, of the forty college libraries indicating a preference for the scope of membership for a centralized processing program, thirty-three, or 82.5 percent, preferred a center for college libraries only. Of the eighty-nine colleges to which the Nelson inquiry was sent, forty-nine, or 60 percent, responded to the question concerning an advantage in centralization on a statewide basis. The response was as follows:

| _Response_[20] | _College Libraries Responding_ | |
| --- | --- | --- |
| | Number | Percent |
| Saw an advantage in centralization of acquisition and processing on a statewide basis | 28 | 72% |
| Saw no advantage | 21 | 43% |

On the basis of these preferences, it can only be concluded that neither school nor college libraries were seeking an alignment or an interrelationship with a multi-type library centralized processing program in New York State.

2) In the _Feasibility_ study relating to the three vast public libraries of New York City, the major recommendation was that "a single cataloging center is proposed to meet the needs of the three public libraries of New York City."[21]

3) Meanwhile, almost simultaneously, the third Nelson study appeared on _Centralized Processing for the Public Libraries of New York State_ which recommended that, "For cataloging and acquisitions, one center is proposed to meet all the public library needs of the state, including those of New York City."[22]

The confusion which the apparently contradictory recommendations could have generated was lessened by the addition of a final recommendation in the New York City study that, "The proposals contained in this report should not be construed as a recommendation that the three libraries of New York City exclude themselves from plans for further centralization of processing among the 22 public library systems of New York State."[23]

There was lacking, then, in the first major recommendation for one center in New York State that it serve multi-type libraries. Despite the preferences indicated both by school and college libraries, however, Nelson Associates recommended without reference to its own findings that, "The reorganized processing and cataloging arrangements should at first serve only the public libraries of the state. Only after the system is operating smoothly should consideration be given to accepting the added volume and other complications implicit in serving other constituencies such as the school libraries."[24]

Since 1966 the systems and State Library have moved quickly toward exploring the formation of one center through the creation of the Association of New York State Libraries for Technical Services, for which a director was appointed in 1968. Deliberate speed seemingly will characterize the implementation of the recommendation that one center be established to meet all the needs of the public libraries in the state.

Currently Arthur D. Little, Inc., looms large in making New York State Library studies, one of which, _A Plan for a Library Processing Center for the State University of New York,_ appeared in 1967. While at least one review advised rejecting the plan because of its superficial qualities, the future of the recommendations remains speculative.[25]

A second Arthur D. Little study also appeared in 1967 and was again limited to a uni-type library. The study, _A Centralized Processing System for School Libraries in New York State,_ endorsed the findings of the Nelson study that school libraries should be involved in a centralized program involving more than one type of library. The recommendation made, however, was that "administrative responsibility for a School Ordering, Cataloging, and Processing (SLOCAP) System" be assigned to the Bureau of School Libraries, New York State Department of Education.[26] The study outlined alternative methods of implementation which could relate the school programs with those either of the public libraries (Association of New York State Libraries for Technical Libraries) or the as yet indeterminate program for the State University of New York.

Amid a bewildering array of such studies and recommendations, to which others could be added, the New York Library Systems structure continues to be remarkably vital, flexible, self-critical, and adventurous, but not yet ready for a commitment to a statewide centralized processing center serving multi-type libraries.

*Recommendations for Pennsylvania.* In Pennsylvania, at the same time the Nelson studies were being made for New York State, the Free Library of Philadephia had requested that a feasibility study be made, the main purpose of which was, "To consider acquisition and centralized processing specifically in terms of service to the Philadelphia Library District, and the potentials for service on a larger service area basis.[27]

The study, which was adopted as a project under the approved Pennsylvania State Plan for the use of Federal Library Services and Construction Act funds, and completed in 1966, includes as a major part an appraisal of some existing programs and/or centers, the findings of which influenced directly the conclusions, the recommendations made to the Philadephia District Library, and the supplementary recommendations made for a statewide program.

The conclusion was that the Philadelphia Library District should not create a centralized processing center for its district alone but rather "That a coordinated plan for a state-wide centralized cataloging and classification program for public libraries should be initiated."[28]

The major recommendation, implying that progress toward such a coordinated plan could be made rather promptly, suggested that the Philadelphia District Library propose that the Pennsylvania State Library: "(A.) Create and subsidize two centralized cataloging and classification centers for public libraries in specified geographic areas. . . . (and,) (B.) Designate each District choosing to contract for the service, as an arterial unit of the cataloging and classification center."[28] Among the duties delineated for each district was the completion of the physical processing of all materials cataloged and classified for the libraries in each district.

While it was beyond the scope of the study to make recommendations to the State Library, two supplementary recommendations proposed that centralized cataloging and classification service or a full processing program be created for academic libraries throughout the state and that a similar centralized processing program be created for school libraries. Since it would have been premature to proceed further with the supplementary recommendations, no procedures for their implementation and no patterns of interrelationships among the programs were proposed in the *Southeastern Pennsylvania Processing Center Feasibility Study.* From the recommendations themselves, however, it can be concluded that the creation of one center serving multi-type libraries was not envisioned as an immediate panacea for the state.

Responses to the recommendation concerning centralized processing for the districts of Pennsylvania have been guarded. Meanwhile, even as a special committee within the state has been considering the recommendations, some of the district libraries, far less prepared than the Philadelphia District Library (the Free Library of Philadelphia) as to resources, staff, and services, have proceeded to offer centralized processing to their member libraries.

In contrast, then, to the developments in New York State where the original plan which fostered centralized processing programs for nineteen of the twenty-two systems has been appraised and found wanting, in Pennsylvania the opposite view has emerged. While the major recommendation for the creation of at least two information flow centers with arterial outlets for the completion of processing details was made to avoid the duplicative programs found in New York State by serving as a deterrent to unilateral district decisions, a preference for district structuring of processing centers has tended to flourish. As of 1968, however, according to the Pennsylvania State Library, the question was not *if* the recommendations were to be implemented but *how best.*

*Recommendations for Louisiana.* A comprehensive evaluation of the total program of library service and library education made for the Louisiana Library Association by John A. Humphry and James Humphry III, appeared in 1968. Specific recommendations in the technical services area can be extracted for the three types of libraries: parish and public, school, and academic.[29]

For parish and public libraries the consultants endorsed a feasibility study made earlier by Marvin W. Mounce that a centralizing processing service for parish and public libraries be established by the State Library. They presented, however, an alternative plan differing from that of Mounce who had recommended a center performing complete processing in that they envisioned decentralization of final processing operations to the library centers of the seven systems which they had recommended for the state.[30]

For school libraries the consultants recommended that: "There be established a state-wide cataloging center for the school libraries under the supervision and administration of the State Supervisor of School Libraries."[31]

For academic libraries the recommendation for college and university libraries including the special libraries of the state was similar to that for school libraries in that it proposed the establishment of a statewide cataloging center. In addition, the consultants anticipated that the "Materials processing centers recommended for each of the seven Library Systems could be utilized by academic libraries as well as by parish libraries."[32]

Like the Pennsylvania recommendations, these for Louisiana envision at least three centers for cataloging and classification by type of library and specifically recommend decentralization of actual processing services to the seven systems when established. The Louisiana recommendation for a coordination of processing services for both academic and parish libraries represents a minimal level of multi-type library service not identified in the Pennsylvania study.

As of late 1968, the Louisiana State Library had assumed the initiative in seeking to implement the recommendation for a centralized processing program for a few parish libraries on an experimental basis.

*Recommendations for Massachusetts.* A recommendation for a total library network challenged the Bureau of Library Extension of the Commonwealth of Massachusetts with the appearance in 1967 of a report entitled *Library Planning Study.*[33] More encompassingly, the report concluded with a projection into the future for the establishment of a New England Regional Library Center. Among the recommendations was that the proposed network: "Create a State Library Service Center, responsible for centralized ordering, cataloging, and processing and the maintenance of a union catalog and union list of serials, which would serve all libraries in the state."[34] It was further recommended that three regional headquarters be created for cataloging and processing services "under the direct supervision of the Bureau of Library Extension and coordinated with the State Library Serivce Center"—the latter of which would centralize all ordering.

Clarification of the responsibilities of the State Library Center and regional headquarters was made in relation to public libraries through a recommendation outlining the procedures in the following manner:

> libraries send book orders to the State Library Service Center, which, in turn, will send orders to the vendors. Because of geographical considerations, vendors will be asked to deliver to the three regional service centers. While the regional service centers are waiting for the books, the state center will prepare catalog cards (using MARC tapes when they become available) according to acceptable library standards. . . . These cards will then be either sent to the regional service center or, more likely, printed out on small supporting units at the regional service centers. When the books arive, they will be processed by the regional service center, matched with the appropriate cards, and sent to the ordering libraries.[35]

With an extension of the services to "all libraries," a commitment to a multi-type library technical service program was thus proposed for the state. Beyond the initial proclamation, however, the report is vague about the attainment of such a service. The following generalized comments from the report concerning college and university libraries, school libraries, and special libraries suggest instead an aura of futurity with such phrases as "will probably want to be encouraged," and "may take part."

Regarding college and university libraries the report states: "Small colleges with limited staff and funds will probably want to take part in this aspect (centralized ordering, cataloging, and processing) of the state library network. Participation would be coordinated through regional offices of the State Library Service Center."[36]

Concerning school libraries the report states: "In school libraries, use of time for book processing is a critical factor, since the library staff often consists of one librarian and, perhaps, one or two student aids." Consequently, a recommendation was made that, "School libraries be encouraged to use the State Library Service Center. The three regional processing centers for all types of libraries will serve the schools. Orders again would be sent to the state center; books would be received, cataloged, processed, and sent out from the appropriate regional office."[37] It was advised that the service be limited to book materials only until the procedures had been tested; later non-book materials were to be added.

The report states that, "Special libraries may take part in the processing activities of the State Service Center, but this would probably be only for standard publications."[38] The report noted, however, that "in its later stages, the center may be able to handle government publications and other specialized material, which would be of value to special libaries."[38]

## Other Types of Libraries

Recommendations for involvement of other types of libraries in the centralized processing program, specifically libraries for the institutionalized and the handicapped were less readily made because the need was less evident when balanced against other internal difficulties and limitations. Since the report surveyed the services of these libraries, however, the following extracts indicate the attention given to technical services and the recommendations that appeared realistic.

*Library Services to the Institutionalized.* While problems of definitions of function; administrative authority; budgets; staff; collections and continuing acquisitional programs; non-written materials and special equipment; and reference services and bibliotheraphy required extensive analysis, technical service problems were minor because many of the collections consisted of donations and discards from other institutions for which minimal cataloging must have been done. Moreover, the thousands of paperbacks which characterize many institutional collections were not cataloged.

Because of the reality of the situation, it was recommended that professional guidance be offered at the state level. The report specifically recommended that two staff positions be created for specialists in institutional libraries within the Bureau of Library Extension. Among the duties delineated for the specialists was: "Maintain liaison with the State Library Service Center to make available to institutional libraries the materials available through the ILL network and reference program."[39]

*Library Services to the Handicapped.* While many organizations serve the handicapped, there are in Massachusetts only two involved with library services: the Massachusetts Commission for the Blind, and Perkins Institute, Watertown. The report concentrated, therefore, on a survey of the handicapped in Massachusetts and of their unique needs for materials and resources. Again, as for the institutional library, technical services were of minor consequence; instead, the following recommendations were made:

> That all special materials, other than Braille, be located at the three regional resource centers in the state, which now serve public libraries but will eventually serve all types of libraries. . . .
> The Bureau of Library Extension should maintain a catalog of all library resources for the handicapped which are held in the state. . . .

This catalog should be reproduced and distributed to all local librarians.[40]

The Massachusetts study recommended in a somewhat more cavalier fashion than did the New York State study that a centralized processing program be created for multi-type library service. There was throughout the report, however, a lessening of emphasis on such a scope and, finally, in the suggested time schedule proposed, centralized processing would begin on a limited basis in the third year after the initial implementation, if any, of the report. Such planning would permit the state to "build staff at Bureau of Library Extension and newly created State Library Center" and to "build system design and program for computer operations."[41]

*Recommendations for Florida.* Unlike the situation in the states previously described, Florida has had a Book Processing Center administered by the Director of the Albertson Public Library of Orlando under a contract between the Orlando Public Library Board and the State Library Board dated November 30, 1961, and amended July 1, 1965. The Center, as of 1968, was serving seventeen library systems in thirty-two of Florida's sixty-seven counties. While the State Library has subsidized processing costs on a decreasing scale for new county and regional libraries, many libraries were not using the services of the Center. The Florida State Library, therefore, financed a study to explore these questions:

Is the present center efficient?

What are the needs—present and future in regard to centralized processing in the state?

How many centers should there be? If more than one appears necessary, what relationships should exist between or among the centers?

What relationships will the State Library have to whatever processing complex is adopted?[42]

While the conclusion was that "the present Center is operating about as efficiently as can be expected of it,"[43] the following recommendations were made that:

1) The Center should be administered by the State Library or be incorporated as a separate agency from the Orlando Public Library with the State Library acting in an advisory position.

2) There is need for a much larger centralized processing effort to be mounted in the State of Florida.

3) The Center should offer the following services:

cataloging only

full processing

ordering but no processing.[44]

As in the Massachusetts study, a recommendation for multi-type library processing services was added: "Processing should be offered to all public libraries and after an initial growth period has elapsed, school libraries and community colleges as well."[44] While no further reference is made in the study to the possible length of "an initial growth period" or to the actual involvement of school and community college libraries, the consultant firm estimated that with the administrative system proposed, the Center would be able "to cope with 500,000 volumes per year—ordered, cataloged, and processed."[45]

As of December 1968, the State Librarian chose between the two obvious and commonly known alternatives concerning the future administration of the Center and endorsed the recommendation that the Center "be administered by the State Library."[46] In so doing, the State Librarian reversed a decision made by one of his predecessors which had predestined the structuring of the Center in Orlando as it had existed.[47]

## THE FUTURE AS VIEWED BY STATE LIBRARIES

The responses being made in the five states to the recommendations and the recommendations themselves, briefly summarized in the preceding section, imply that the trend is indeed toward statewide centralization of technical services. Of the forty-two state libraries which provided data on centralized processing developments within their states, thirty-one, or 74 percent indicated that they were concerned with planning for the future. Twelve of the state libraries noted that they had had some kind of feasibility study made or were currently involved with such a study.

The following developments, reported by six state libraries, typify the variant approaches being made to the rapidly solidifying concept of statewide centralized processing. The innovative and personalized adaptations which characterize the approaches offer assurance that, despite the conformal and repetitive recommendations found in many of the surveys and feasibility studies, the state libraries assert individualized and viable leadership in planning both as to scope of technical service programs and to type of library or libraries for which the service is to be available.

While the California State Library Processing Center now serves public libraries only, plans are being made for the establishment of an automated center for cooperative cataloging and for serials control. The services of the center are to be available to any type of library. A pilot project is scheduled to begin in 1970.

The Connecticut State Library is planning the establishment of a centralized processing center initially for public libraries only. Ultimately, the services of the center are to be available "to any in-state library."[48]

The Hawaii State Library, in part because of unique environmental factors, has been more successful than any state in its near instant implementation of its plans for centralization of complete processing of materials, book and nonbook, for public and school libraries. Aware of the success, the State Librarian, having concluded that "cooperation is at its maximum" within his state boundaries, seeks to extend his program beyond Hawaii's shores, for, according to him, he has been actively

> negotiating with the Territory of Guam, the American Trust Territory, and with American Samoa to see if we cannot cooperate with them, or they with us, in the purchasing and processing of books. . . .Hopefully,

in fiscal 1969, we will have a Pan Pacific processing center in operation.[48]

Should the plan become operative, Hawaii will be able to demonstarte to the mainland states the potential of planning within flexible geographical perimeters—beyond inflexible state boundaries.

The Minnesota State Library is contemplating the development of statewide cooperative activities between types of libraries, especially through the use of a union catalog and book catalogs.

The Nevada State Library now has as one of its divisions in operation the Nevada Center for Cooperative Library Services. The Center encourages multitype library participation through its services to public, school, and institutional libraries. The services are available to any library to the extent that facilities permit.

The Washington State Library plans to produce book catalogs of member libraries within designated geographical areas. Acceptance of centralized cataloging services is, however, to be optional.

While it would be possible, though perhaps presumptive, to make recommendations to the state of Illinois on the basis of the evidence presented, it is necessary that the self-appraisal be made by Illinois librarians themselves. It seems appropriate, therefore, to conclude with questions which, it is hoped, will generate answers and further probing by a state exploring its commitment to a multi-type library membership in a centralized technical services program.

The following questions relate to: 1) establishing an inquiry concerning statewide centralization of technical services, 2) characteristics of centralized technical service programs, 3) the member library in a statewide network, 4) the center/centers in a statewide network, 5) membership, 6) human resource adaptability/technological feasibility, and 7) beyond statewide involvement.

## QUESTIONS

1. *Toward an inquiry concerning statewide centralization of technical services*
   a. What can be learned from a study of statewide library surveys and recommendations that have already been made?
   b. What has been the repetitive pattern both in selection of the surveyors and of the recommendations made thus far?
   c. Has the time come for librarians in a state to challenge the traditional acclamation for the objectivity represented by impersonalism? Is it better to be biased for sound reasons than purposefully vacuous?
   d. Should a self-analysis—not just for technical services but for a comprehensive statewide program—be made by librarians within a state, by consultants within the profession, or by commercial firms?

2. *Characteristics of centralized technical service programs*
   a.    *Scope* — What should be the scope of services to be offered?
      1)    Acquisition

2) Acquisition and cataloging data (information data)
3) Acquisition, cataloging data, processing, and delivery
4) Cataloging data (information data)
5) Cataloging data, processing, and delivery
6) Other

b. *Kinds of materials*
1) Should the center assume responsibility for all materials whatever the format?
2) Should the center limit its services to *book* format?
3) Should there be a progressive extension of services to include all formats?
4) What is the consequence if the center does not assume responsibility for all formats?
5) If a local library must or does retain a catalog department, what should be its relationship with the center?
6) What kinds of materials could be acquired by member libraries without the necessity of maintaining a separate catalog department?

c. *Selection of library resources*
1) To what extent should the center become involved with selection?
2) Is there any advantage of simultaneous ordering of the same title by member libraries? Does the advantage outweigh the possible disadvantages?

d. *Analysis*
1) Should a new level of analysis of content be considered or is the present level satisfactory?
2) Does the computer make possible—for the first time—the reality of more detailed analysis of the content of resources for multi-type use?
3) If member libraries are not willing to accept a common policy for descriptive analysis, subject headings, and classification, should further self-appraisal be made by such a member library before participating?

e. *Catalog data*
1) Enumerate the advantages and disadvantages of book and card catalog formats.
2) Should a book catalog format be preferred as a psychological deterrent to the compulsion to tinker with data on a 3'' x 5'' catalog card?
3) What new formats for recording and making data available are emerging which may make obsolete both the book and card catalog formats?

       4)    Should emphasis in member libraries be first on the data and secondly on the techniques for recording?

   f.   *Responsibility for resource availability*
      1)    Does the center or the member library assume responsibility for maintaining the card catalog, the book catalog, or the inventory of local resources?
      2)    Does statewide planning assume statewide availability of resources?
      3)    What liaison relationships can be established between/among member libraries and the center?

3.   *The member library in a statewide network*

   a.   What are the advantages and disadvantages inherent in the acceptance of centralized technical services by an autonomous local library? By a local library as a member of a system?

   b.   If abandonment of certain local policies is considered a disadvantage, to what extent is adhering to such policies a fetish rather than reasonable?

   c.   What responsibilities could be transferred readily to a center and what must the member library retain?

   d.   What relations would involvement in a statewide network foster between a local library and the State Library?

   e.   What would be the new administrative structuring and new positions created within a library which could abandon completely or re-design its technical services department?

   f.   What new or expanded services are to be offered by a local library which can allocate time formerly devoted to technical services to such new services? If none have been anticipated, is a library ready for participation?

   g.   What are the philosophical and pragmatic reasons which would prompt or deter a library's participation in a centralized processing program?

4.   *The center/centers in a statewide network*

   a.   What effect will the decision concerning the scope of centralized services have on the organization and administration of a center or centers?

b.   Does technological expertise make passé the necessity of *total* processing within a center?

c.   Would one center performing complete processing be preferable to one concerned with acquisition and information flow?

d.   If processing outlets/depots are scattered throughout a state, what should be the administrative relations to the center and to each member library?

e.   In a state with a developed library systems structure, what problems emerge if each system which originally offered centralized processing to its members seeks to implement a recommendation for fewer—perhaps one—center in a state?

f.   What problems, administrative, organizational, financial, staffing, are to be encountered in statewide planning for one or more centers?

g.   What are to be the responsibility and involvement of the state library in statewide planning such as for centralization of technical services?

5.   *Membership*

a.   What factors contributed to the original planning of centers for uni-type libraries?

b.   Does statewide planning invite/compel consideration of multi-type library membership? Why?

c.   Have the problems thus far encountered in centralized processing programs limited to *uni*-type library membership been solved?

d.   Would they have been more readily solved with a *multi*-type library membership?

e.   Should *multi*-type library membership be sought simultaneously or as the services are proved effective through an extension beyond one type?

f.   Should *uni*-type library membership centers be created simultaneously but so designed and administered that unification could be attained through progressive phases of interaction?

g. Could there be centralized administration within a center having divisions for *uni*-type membership sharing common resources, such as bibliographies, MARC tape, computers, etc.?

6. *Human resource adaptability/technological feasibility*

a. Is technological feasibility enough?

b. Should not technological feasibility, however sophisticated the technology, be accompanied by the conventional wisdom that the staffs of member libraries not only be receptive to changes engendered by technology but also creative in exploring new dimensions of reader/user services?

c. Should there be a preliminary period for the breaking of barriers, often encrusted with compliance and complacency, which could impede the most brilliantly conceived statewide program?

d. If such barriers prove invulnerable, if there is no receptivity, no readiness for a new concept of library services emanating from a local library, can a centralized program really succeed?

7. *Beyond statewide involvement. . .*

a. Identify the existing subject information network services in the United States.

b. Should there be continuing recognition of the potential nationwide linking of information data sources in any current statewide planning?

Some contribution to the "beginnings of a state plan for library services in Illinois" may result from the responses to these and other questions. Whatever the plan, those librarians of Illinois who encounter impediments to its development or are impediments themselves will recognize the enduringly perceptive and pragmatic appraisal of the librarian's readiness for involvement made long ago by Melvil Dewey:

The simpl explanation is that many librarians hav not yet wakened to understand how great a movement is going on and how rapidly old conditions and standards ar giving way to new. They ar carried forward by the tide, but not without kicking and splashing; and yet curiously sum of these very pepl ar most self-satisfied to find themselves so far advanst and quite oblivious that every step was takn not from pressure within impelling them to go forward and help the workers but from pressure without. Their hands wer tied to the car of progress but other hands gav it its momentum and they insted of dragging it hav been dragged by it. Every great movement is handicapt in this way and we ar happy abuv the average in having only opposition that like a brake on a hevy down grade simply insures that our car runs more stedily, safely, and surely to its goal. We ar stong enuf now to signal "brakes off" or, like the baloonist, to throw out sand bags when we no longer need their ballast.[49]

## References

1. "Cooperation." In *Random House Dictionary of the English Language.* New York, Random House. Vol. 3, 1967, p. 321.

2. Vann, Sarah K. "Evaluation of Centers: the Views of Members," *Library Trends,* 16:23-45, July 1967.

3. *Southeastern Pennsylvania Processing Center Feasibility Study. Final Report* (Pennsylvania State Library Monograph No. 4). By Sarah K. Vann. Sponsored by the Philadelphia District Library Center (Free Library of Philadelphia. Harrisburg, Department of Public Instruction. Pennsylvania State Library, 1967.

4. For a copy of the questionnarie for the "Survey of Processing Centers in the United States," see *Ibid,* pp. 156-159. For data on membership as noted, see *Ibid.,* p. 57.

5. Bundy, Mary Lee. *Public Library Processing Centers: a Report of a Nationwide Survey.* Troy, N.Y., 1962, p. 40.

6. Quoted in *Southeastern Pennsylvania Processing Center Feasibility Study, op. cit.,* p. 58.

7. Georgia. State Catalog Service. *Annual Report, 1967-68.*Atlanta, 1968. (Typed copy.)

8. Data from James R. Hunt, State Librarian, Honolulu, Hawaii.

9. Letter of August 12, 1968, from James R. Hunt, State Librarian, Honolulu, Hawaii.

10. *Southeastern Pennsylvania Processing Center Feasibility Study, op. cit.,* p. 35.

11. *Ibid.,* p. 37.

12. *Ibid.,* p. 38.

13. U.S. Office of Education. *Statewide Long-Range Planning for Libraries.* Report of Conference (September 19-22, 1965) Chicago, Illinois. Sponsored by Library Services Branch. Edited by Herbert A. Carl. Washington, U.S.G.P.O., 1966, p. 50.

14. *Ibid.*

15. *Ibid.,* p. 12.

16. Rike, Galen E. *Statewide Library Surveys and Development Plans: an Annotated Bibliography.* Springfield, Illinois State Library, 1968.

17. *Ibid.,* p. v.

18. Florida. State Library. *Centralized Processing for the State of Florida.* Boston, Arthur D. Little, 1968.

19. New York. State Library. *Feasibility of School and College Library Processing Through Public Library Systems in New York State.* A Report for the New York State Library. New York, Nelson Associates, 1966, p. 3.

20. *Ibid.,* pp. 3-4.

21. *The Feasibility of Further Centralizing the Technical Processing Operations of the Public Libraries of New York City.* A survey conducted for the Brooklyn Public Library, the New York Public Library and the Queens Borough Public Library. New York, Nelson Associations in collaboration with the Theodore Stein Company, 1966, p. 1.

22. New York. State Library. *Centralized Processing for the Public Libraries of New York State.* A survey conducted for the New York State Library. New York, Nelson Associates in collaboration with the Theodore Stein Company, 1966, p. 1.

23. *The Feasibility of Further Centralizing the Technical Processing Operations of the Public Libraries of New York City, op. cit.,* p. ii.

24. New York. State Library. *Centralized Processing for the Public Libraries of New York State, op. cit.,* p. 2.

25. Critical appraisal made by Sarah K. Vann, November 26, 1967. (Unpublished.)

26. New York. Education Department. Bureau of School Libraries. *A Centralized Processing System for School Libraries in New York State.* Report to Bureau of School Libraries, New York State Education Department. Boston, Arthur D. Little, 1967, p. 2.

27. *Southeastern Pennsylvania Processing Center Feasibility Study, op cit.,* p. ix.

28. *Ibid.,* p. 1.

29. Louisiana Library Association. *Library Service in Louisiana; Keeping Pace with Progress in the State.* A Report prepared for the Louisiana Library Association, by John A. Humphry and James Humphry III. New York, 1968. For background information on the development of parish libraries, see Chapter iii, "Parish and Public Library Service."

30. *Ibid.,* p. 59.

31. *Ibid.,* p. 99.

32. *Ibid.,* p. 103.

33. Massachusetts. Bureau of Library Extension. *Library Planning Study.* Report to the Bureau of Library Extension, Department of Education, Commonwealth of Massachusetts. Boston, Arthur D. Little, 1967.

34. *Ibid.,* p. 2.

35. *Ibid.,* pp. 24-25.

36. *Ibid.,* p. 26.

37. *Ibid.,* pp. 28-29.

38. *Ibid.,* p. 31.

39. *Ibid.,* p. 52.

40. *Ibid.,* p. 69.

41. *Ibid.,* p. 6.

42. Florida State Library. *Centralized Processing in the State of Florida.* Boston, Arthur D. Little, 1968, p. 1.

43. *Ibid.,* p. 32.

44. *Ibid.,* p. 3.

45. *Ibid.,* p. 48.

46. Telephone conversation with F. William Summers, December 5, 1968.

47. Southeastern Pennsylvania Processing Center Feasibility Study, *op cit.*, p. 35.

48. Responses, slightly paraphrased, to a letter of July 15, 1968.

49. Dewey, Melvil *Library Notes*, 2:288, March 1888.

Donald E. Wright
*Librarian, Evanston Public Library*
*Evanston Illinois*

# COOPERATION BETWEEN TYPES OF
# LIBRARIES IN ILLINOIS TODAY

My responsibility at this conference is "to review all known main instances of such cooperation (between libraries of different types) in the past and in the present, with a critical evaluation of their results, to present a projection of what you think might be the next steps to take in this direction." Taken literally, then, my role has become one of historian, critic, and prophet. I will not attempt to fill these roles, for to do so would presume an exhaustive study on my part and assure an exhaustive afternoon on your part.

I will, however, attempt to fulfill this assignment in some degree. Let me begin by telling you what I have done in preparation for this meeting. Through *Illinois Libraries,* I have reviewed library literature for references to Illinois library cooperation. A questionnaire was mailed to over 500 librarians in the state and personal conversations were held with several librarians. With the above as a basis I shall report on the literature search and the questionnaire, report in some detail on certain cooperative programs as defined by this program, and offer some comments.

A review of periodical indexes was made in an attempt to identify activities between various types of libraries which could be classified as inter-library cooperation in Illinois. None were found which truly cut across library lines. This is, of course, not conclusive evidence that nothing has been done—it is only an indication that nothing has been written which was then indexed. Often, however, library literature does not adequately represent projects or activities which are truly working and innovative.

In a second attempt to identify projects within Illinois, a search through *Illinois Libraries* was made. It was both an interesting and frightening task to review the past forty or so years in Illinois libraries—frightening in that it raises many questions as to what has been accomplished in this state and in the profession. This review of literature then did not produce tangible leads to projects which cut across library lines in the interest of better library service. There were, to be sure, several articles on school and public libraries working together, but these were the familiar song and dance routines which go something like the following: teachers come to tea at public library; children's librarian speaks to teachers; public library has story hour and summer reading program; and teachers do not tell anyone (school librarians or public librarians) about assignments. Thus in perusal of the periodical which should reflect Illinois librarianship and library development, no good clues were found which would direct one to interlibrary activities.

The second step to gain information was a questionnaire. In early August 1968, a questionnaire was sent to over 500 libraries in Illinois. It was sent to all public libraries, selected school libraries, all university and college libraries, and selected special librarians. Two hundred and ninety-six returns were received. The questionnaire was very brief and was designed only to lead me to interlibrary experiences. Five questions were asked and followed a brief cover letter which stated the purpose of the questionnaire. The five questions were:

1. Check the type of library you represent. (Various types were listed with a space to check the one applicable.)

2. Has your library participated in any joint acitivity with another library during the past ten years?
   Yes or No

3. If yes, identify the other type(s) of library(ies) involved:
   Public          College          University
   School          Special          Other

4. Characterize briefly the key action involved. (For example, "shared staff," "joint reference selection," "joint periodical pool," etc.)

5. Have you made any efforts to discuss or to plan cooperative activities with other librarians without success? Yes or No. If yes, what types of activities were being proposed?

One hundred and seventy-five of the questionnaires returned answered "no" to questions two and five. No activity between their library and another library was in force and none had been tried the past ten years. This was a flat "no" to both questions.

Several of the respondents indicated cooperation between their library and an agency of the same type. This is especially true in relationship to the new public library systems. Many public librarians checked the questionnaire to indicate that they, a public library, cooperated with another type of library and identified that as a library system. This is an interesting situation in which the members of an organization indicate their gratefulness for the cooperation the system was established to generate and hold up their cooperative spirit as an emblem of achievement when the other party on the line is, in fact, their creature. This fact may well indicate a barrier to interlibrary activity if our basic structure lines are not clear and understood by librarians.

Examples of cooperation with other libraries of the same type are what could be generally expected. Some examples of cooperation between public libraries follow: host to library laboratory; host to district meeting for State Library; book exhibits; loans from the Illinois State Library; exchange of mysteries, science fiction, westerns, etc.; amnesty days; courtesy cards; shared lists of periodicals; essay and general literature index responsibility; exchange of gifts and duplicates; exchange of ideas; and periodical meetings of librarians.

There were two activities noted as having been discussed or tried between public libraries without success: a community card program between six neighboring libraries (three libraries are doing it) and reciprocal cards between four suburban libraries.

From the questionnaire, college libraries in Illinois appear to be cooperating the most with one another. A sampling of their activities follow: union list of serials for twenty-eight college libraries; equal access to resources of another college; joint periodical list; regular delivery schedule between two campuses; teletype network; supplying of photocopies for mutilated periodicals; exchange new accessions lists; cooperative purchasing; and shared staff and materials. No school librarians responded to this question with examples. However, it is known that some school systems have cooperative programs with other school libraries of the nature noted.

Let us turn our attention to the examples of interlibrary cooperation revealed on the questionnaire.

1) Public library and school library cooperation. There are no startling revelations or challenging stimulators among the actions identified. Here is a sampling of responses:

> reserve shelf at public library for school assignments
> public library visits by schools
> library instruction to classes
> classroom collections to schools
> joint amnesty day
> cooperative book return
> joint periodical pool
> shared cataloging tools
> provide junior high with paperbound *Reader's Guide*
> help high school students with research
> shared staff
> shared administration and operation
> joint book selection meetings
> regular exchange of lists of periodical holdings and new book
>     acquisitions
> attend library meetings together
> borrow reference books from one another
> informal discussion group of librarians within area

joint facilities
(This only in one instance and in that it is one of common administration with more than one administrative board.)
an Articulation Committee composed of "administrations of public library and local schools (public and parochial); key library people (public and school); representatives of teaching staff"
exchange of bibliographies
bookmobile to schools
participate in career day
publication of local library directory
school librarian helped to catalog our books
joint National Library Week program
joint use of film collections
joint radio program

2) Public libraries and colleges and universities. Again the following is a quick identification:

interlibrary loans
National Library Week cooperation
cooperative exhibits
honor university library cards
share staff—small college and small public library
joint reference selection
joint use of quarters (new junior colleges)
microfilm pool of local newspapers
joint use of LTP reports
joint purchases of certain collections
    (such as essay and general literature indexed items)
cheaper non-resident cards for college students

It is interesting to note that one public library indicated extensive cooperation with its neighboring university library—but that university listed none.

3) Public libraries and special libraries:

interlibrary loans
sends specialized material to special library—receives general materials

This is not a long list of activities but it does represent the activities reported. You can see that there is some interlibrary activity in practice. There is probably more which did not come into evidence during the survey but what was given is representative enough to show clearly the present patterns.

Answers to the last question provided indications of activities which were tried but failed. Only a dozen replies indicated that overtures had been made in a certain direction to no avail. They included:

reciprocal use of a school film collection by a public library (which loaned theirs to the school)

schools wanted to use our films but policy did not permit

improved conversation with schools on assignments

extension of borrowing privileges to junior college students via an area common library card

complete cataloging of public library books in the school library

and vice versa, cataloging of school library collection by the public library

joint acquisition and service policy statement between libraries of several types (failed because of suspicion on part of schools and special libraries)

shared use of reference materials

tried to arrange a liberal interloan with a special library but to no avail

tried college library to exchange shelflists with the public library but insufficient funds

And these final three frustrated plans of a junior college librarian:

tried to get a joint book catalog between several junior colleges but staffs didn't want it

tried (junior college library) to join the processing center but they couldn't cope with a college—only small public libraries

tried to work with LIBRA, but they, naturally, wish to cooperate with institutions like themselves—small four-year liberal arts colleges

Two activities which have cut across library lines and are representative of what activity has been taken included the establishment of an association or organization for discussion and action and a cooperative effort between a school and a public library. An Articulation Committee has been formed in one city with the following purpose: to establish communication channels and lines for action between public and school and special library programs. The committee includes the following representation: the director of the public library, superintendent of public schools, chief administrator for parochial schools, a representative of the school principals' council, school reading specialists, two special librarians, and department heads from the public library. This group meets twice a year and committees, when needed, are formed to achieve certain action. Although the public librarian feels discouraged at times, he believes that it is a worthwhile project and one which is productive. It has opened up communication with school officials and three top school administrators have become library conscious.

The public librarian would like to see a coordinated selection policy for all publicly supported library units within the community. This has not been achieved to date because of suspicion or uncertainty on the part of the school officials. While the school board could impose such, the public librarian hopes it will come about through mutual trust and understanding.

Another example of interlibrary cooperation referred to above has been used for many years as an example of public and school cooperation—I refer to the relationship between the Evanston Public Library and the Evanston elementary schools. I am reporting on it in some detail because it offers, I believe, some interesting lessons in cooperation. The boards of the Evanston Public Library and of the elementary school district have had a long, interesting relationship— referred to quite often as a cooperative system.

Although this cooperative system was formally organized in 1921, classroom collections had been provided by the Public Library as early as 1896. Each classroom was allotted three-month loans of twenty books which school boys transported between the Public Library and the schools in small carts. Teachers were enthusiastic about this opportunity for encouraging good reading habits. At this time, the schools were providing only general reference books. Marian Lindsay, the librarian of the Public Library, believed that school libraries should be maintained by the Public Library to provide greater book strength through interchange of books. Public demand for more library service for adults, as well as children, resulted in the establishment of deposit stations in two schools. These stations, which were open one afternoon and evening each week, provided books for children and adults.

In 1918, the Mother's Clubs established special memorial library rooms in honor of school principals in two elementary schools. These libraries stimulated interest and desire for a separate library in every elementary school. In 1921, the Juul law, a state law which reduced the Public Library budget by one third, made it impossible to continue library service to the schools. The board of education was fully aware of the value of school libraries and was ready to accept the library board's program for cooperative financing and service to the schools.

As the first step in this cooperative plan, the two boards jointly employed a trained and experienced children's librarian who was to devote half time to supervising children's services at the Public Library and half time to supervising school libraries. As a member of the Public Library staff, she administered the children's department and selected and purchased all children's books. As an employee of the school board, she was given the right of a supervisor to enter classrooms to talk about books and give instruction on the use of the library.

An outstanding development of Public Library and school cooperation was the establishment of centralized cataloging. A specialist was employed to catalog, classify, and maintain a master shelflist of all books acquired by the schools or the children's department of the Public Library. This method of cooperative cataloging provided a uniform system of cataloging. With the exception of two schools, library books were placed in classrooms and serviced by the classroom teacher. The supervisor visited each class once a month.

When the Boltwood Intermediate School opened in 1924, the first full time school librarian was employed jointly by the two boards. The school board paid two-thirds of her salary, while the library board paid one-third. This librarian, who had both teacher and library science background, assigned classes to a weekly period in the library for instruction in the use of books and catalogs and book appreciation. This experimental step in cooperation between school and library boards was highly successful.

Several new school libraries were established within the next few years. In 1926, the Foster School garage was turned into a library. The new Haven

Intermediate School, built in 1927, had a special library room with a full time librarian. In 1928, Willard School established a separate library room. In 1929, an itinerant librarian was employed to assist the supervisor. This same year school library cards were replaced by juvenile public library cards which could be used in the school library, the main library, or a branch library.

This same year, the two school boards (prior to the present District 65, there were two elementary school districts) agreed that the school library rooms which could be used as community libraries would be provided in each new school. By 1933 this plan had been carried out, and thirteen of the fourteen elementary schools had a separate library room. Each class was assigned to at least one library period each week. Six librarians, with education and library science degrees, served these schools.

By 1939, the staff included nine librarians, the number increasing as new schools were built. The Public Library paid one-third of the salary of most of the school librarians, as well as one-half of the salary of the supervisor. In May, 1945, the library board revised the policy concerning the relationship between the library and the two school boards. Through the growth of traveling branch service and the opening of a separate north branch (a south branch had been established many years earlier), the schools no longer served as branches, and school librarians devoted their entire time to school library service. Therefore, the two boards agreed that the schools would pay the full salary of the school librarians. The following quotation, from a statement by the library board at that time, indicates the philosophy of service to school children:

> We do not, in any way, wish to alter the fine spirit of cooperation and mutual agreement that has so long been enjoyed by the library and the schools and which has worked to produce so many benefits and advantages. Because of the mutual understanding of the School Boards and the Library Board on the necessity for and value of our past cooperative venture in the joint operation of the libraries concerned, we feel, in adopting this permanent policy, that the School Boards of Districts 75 and 76 and the Library Board should go on record in expressing their wish and desire that no action be taken in the future that might endanger or lead to its dissolution.

Since 1945, there have been many areas of continued cooperation between the Public Library and the schools; i.e., book selection and purchasing, cataloging and a union shelflist, processing, interlibrary loan, registration of all children providing a common borrower's card, and delivery service which makes it possible for children to return library books at any agency. The coordinator or supervisor, whose salary was until this year shared equally by the school board and the Public Library, supervises the librarians in the twenty-one school libraries and the materials center as well as the children's department of the Public Library.

Greatly increased enrollment in the schools and changes in policies of school administration have affected the Public Library's role in the cooperative plan. Prior to the employment of a special school personnel director, the director of the public library, together with the supervisor (or coordinator) of school libraries, initiated contact with and interviewed all applicants for school library positions. The school business manager has assumed responsibility for budget planning and purchase of equipment, etc. With increasing school library development and expanded material purchasing assisted by the various federal programs, there was a gradual shift from a coordinated operation to separate but physically adjacent operations.

Today Evanston has a cooperative system although very different from that envisioned by Marian Lindsay in the 1920's. Was separation of the technical process and the shared staff necessary? It appears that the separation of certain operations of technical processing came about because of the inability of the Public Library unit to respond to the increased load of school materials. In part, there was a non-acceptance by the Public Library of the plan to shorten catalog entries for certain children's material.

The last of the shared staff was the coordinator. The nature of this position has changed and I feel it is an important change since a full time, high level coordinator of children's services is needed, just as the schools need the undivided attention of their supervisor. Cooperation still is done on some fronts—such as the technical processing of school materials is done at the Public Library by a school staff with shared resources; there is a single charging system throughout the Public Library and elementary schools giving the child fewer routines and rules with which to become familiar; delivery service between all units permits free interchange of books; and our children's librarian attends all school library staff meetings and vice versa. Evanston is increasing its effectiveness through a true cooperative program which is still developing as the old dependency and not too clearly defined program is retired.

There seem to me to be certain problems—possibly inherent—in the profession which can stifle us. There were clear and distinct indications that "size of library" and "distance" will still serve as an argument or excuse for lack of action or inaction. This is an age-old problem which apparently logic and positive and constructive examples cannot solve. These excuses were used time after time as a reason for "no" replies—but, perhaps, it is encouraging that persons felt compelled to excuse their negative reply. Perhaps cooperation has become a mode, if not a manner, and with it, at least in the vocabulary, we have hope.

Other barriers which could be enumerated can be summed up in one word—and that same word notes our greatest resource—"people." This means that we are either in great shape—or we really have problems. So many of the problems enumerated come back to the people involved: the school librarians who would not cooperate; the board which vetoed the idea; the public librarians who did not want to serve students. If we are to utilize our greatest resource, we are going to need to achieve an orientation to total library service. All types of librarians, library school faculty, library trustees—all who are concerned with the library universe—must be oriented to service and to each type of library's primary purpose.

If we are deterred by such things as "distance," "size," "reciprocal borrowing" and so forth, perhaps our basic problem is people. Only one person mentioned this in his reply and his complaint was "lack of help keeps us from doing things like this." I suspect he was referring to cooperative activities but the meaning is unclear, as are many of our arguments or protests against inaction or ignorance.

There are, I think, some commendable and profitable activities going on in Illinois. We seem unable, though, to make relatively simple relationships. Many of us fight reciprocal borrowing today—and hope to dip into those troubled waters with someone else's toe—we will start with a pilot program and build gradually. We are unable to accept the testimony and experiences of others in our own state and region—or even experts from New York. Just as we are unable to accept and apply the experience factor of others in this regard, we are unable to accept the usefulness across types of library lines of such things as union lists of serials, interlibrary loan, centralized periodical pool, and so on.

We seem not only to lack imagination but to lack a certain enthusiasm or initiative. The single activity which was noted with the most frequency as an interlibrary activity was interlibrary loan. The interesting fact in this regard is that in over 70 percent of those replies noting public library-system cooperation it was interlibrary loan which was held up as the example of service. As a profession we have had the mechanics of interlibrary loan for some time. Why have we not noticed it? Did we lack the imagination to tap the source or, did we need a simpler method? My library certainly did not engage in interlibrary lending until pushed to the brink by a patron—but now we are the tenth busiest user out of a field of twenty-eight in our system's interloan business.

Finally, there was a definite categorizing of libraries and library users in the replies to the questionnaire. Libraries were thought of as a certain type and any service given was given to a type of patron. In enough instances that it could be considered a pattern, there was evidence that a student belonged in a school library or a university or college library. When he came to the public library he came to alien ground and there was philanthropy involved in the service, if any was given.

Are we unable to think in broad service patterns? I realize the facts of life and the necessity for a certain definition in relationship to our source of funds but, do we not need to define our roles also in terms of broad service patterns rather than in a limiting way? Somewhere, somehow, we must achieve an orientation to service.

If librarians tend to categorize they also tend to shy from responsibility. And this is, it seems to me, a barrier. Several persons noted specific examples in which a project was not started or failed because someone did not accept responsibility—including, evidently, the person making the charge. It appears that we are either on such tenuous ground or made of such weak material that we are unable to exercise a leadership or coordinating role. I seriously question the life expectancy of a state plan which is dependent upon a group so oriented to leadership or commitment roles.

I was asked to comment upon possible next steps toward a state plan, and I will make only two comments in this regard. The first refers to the legal structure for library service within Illinois and the second refers to our positive resources in Illinois. I am confident that attention must be given to the legal structure of library responsibility in Illinois. I am not referring alone to the place of the Illinois State Library in the state structure. I have always maintained that the structure of library service in a state need not be a determining factor in the character of that service. However, I would list the legal structure as a barrier to the development of a state plan for two reasons, the number of groups—official and otherwise—which serve in various capacities the official state organization and the lack of comprehensive or total responsibility within one agency or compatible agencies. Let us look at the public library pattern. We have a legally constituted Advisory Committee to the Illinois State Library. In addition to the official Advisory Committee, we have an Advisory Council with several sub-committees, each concerned with a part of the federal Library Services and Construction Act. Indeed, the Title III subcommittee was formed expressly to be concerned with the type of library cooperation I have discussed. We also have the Illinois Library Association's Library Development Committee which has served a variety of functions, and served them admirably. With the library systems we begin a new series of committees or groups working in various advisory capacities to the state agency.

Is it impossible for the state agency to communicate effectively and to act responsively to so many groups and is it necessary? The existence of so many groups when not adequately informed or directed can create misunderstanding and misadventures; and it has done so.

It seems to me that as a corps of professionals we librarians should not need to seek such unions or multiply with such indiscretion the number of groups which purport to represent special interests or serve special purposes. I feel that instead of creating or building a strong central unit through our legal advisory committee, we are merely constructing temporary supports. There is also the fact that responsibility for library service for schools, public libraries, junior colleges, and universities is lodged either in separate agencies and coordination is at best tenuous, or statutory responsibility is lacking or hazy.

I would encourage the State Library Advisory Committee to assume an aggressive leadership role in state development. This unit is the only group with legal implication and is the group with authority over the Title III funds. This Advisory Committee could coordinate activities within the state; it could consolidate the activities and work of its own state library agency; it could begin to build that agency to the point where the staff and the services command the respect not only of the library community but of the entire state. I believe this is the group that needs our support and our active help—this is the group that could make a difference in Illinois library service.

We have a great deal going for us in Illinois which should prove of help in our attempt to develop a comprehensive library plan. We have:

> three accredited library schools
> a fairly substantial professional membership association
> active special library associations and a fairly complete series of local or regional library groups
> a developing public library system which could provide a key to coordination and encouragement (But a word of caution here. We—the profession—have organized the state into public library systems and, for

the most part, we are pleased at our performance. It appears that this will offer a convenient channel for communication and for action. It could, however, also be a barrier to development. While we recognize and admire the abilities of those who have been attracted to our system staffs, the official groups in the state must remember that these are not the only librarians in the state and efforts must be made to work with the public and school librarians—on the local level. This is where representative librarianship is—and this is where support for future state programs rests.)

excellent library resources among our universities, special libraries, school libraries, etc.

a group of concerned librarians who are willing to help and have the abilities which could make a difference in state dvelopment

a library climate which was able to accomplish legislation and aid for public libraries in a remarkably short time

Certainly we need a comprehensive plan for library development in Illinois. From my observation and study we have not taken advantage of the opportunities we have had, and we need not be either overly impressed or depressed by our past. We need to have prime concern for the future.

Carolyn Crawford
*Director, School Libraries
and Instructional Materials
Department of Education
Hawaii*

# COOPERATION BETWEEN SCHOOL LIBRARIES
# AND OTHER TYPES OF LIBRARIES

Since I come from a Hawaii, a state with a unique centralized system, perhaps I should begin by taking a look at its organizational pattern of school and other types of libraries.[1] In Hawaii, public libraries were placed in the reorganized State Department of Education following statehood. While this is not unusual at the municipal level its uniqueness lies in the fact that Hawaii has a true statewide system. It includes the State Library, all public libraries, all public school libraries and the Central Processing Center. Each of these branches is under a director who is responsible to the state librarian whose rank is that of an assistant superintendent.

There is one board of education in Hawaii, but there are no local boards; the state board members are elected from geographical regions. This is the policy making and governing body of the library system with two members serving as a Library Committee. For each of the seven school districts, there is an Education Advisory Council, appointed by the governor. There are four Library Advisory Commissions, also appointive, which are an inheritance from the pre-statehood autonomous county library system. Both Council and Commission members serve in an advisory capacity only, but they do play an important role in the planning of educational and library programs.

Since all funds come from taxes, the state legislature acts as a governing body to the degree that it controls the budget. For example, in the appropriation bill which established central processing it was stipulated that the center would serve both school and public libraries.

47

As joint operations developed, there has been on the one hand a consistent effort to define our diverse roles, to cut down on duplication of effort and to provide for joint long range planning and, on the other hand, emphasis on the use of all types of "carriers of knowledge" regardless of type of library. Objectives in serving the total population are to provide exciting experiences in learning, to make available our entire cultural heritage, to provide a rich collection of materials and to make use of modern technological aids. It is true that this system represents an intra-departmental structure for school and public libraries; however, working from such a base, Hawaii has made progress in terms of interlibrary cooperation.

Two general observations should be made at this point: first, cooperation as a term implies give and take—when the giving is entirely on one side it is not cooperation; second, when talking about cooperation between types of libraries, we should remember that in many cases the different types are competing for the same tax dollar.

Turning to the national scene, we could examine cooperative ventures in which schools are involved through several approaches: the historical, the geographical or by type. While it is not my purpose to give a re-hash of historical development, certain landmarks need to be mentioned. A good bibliography on the very early period may be found in the January 1953 issue of *Library Trends*.[2] As early as 1901 there appeared an article in *Library Journal* entitled "Co-operation between Libraries and Schools: An Historical Sketch," by Josephine Rathbone.[3] No doubt most of the "cooperation" during that early period was one directional. By the 1920's there was considerable school library development in various sections of the country. The depression days of the 1930's impeded progress although the bookmobile or other means of service were offered schools by the public libraries: this continued in many areas through the war years and into the second half of the century.

With Sputnik and the consequent knowledge explosion, there came an invasion of public, college and university libraries by students. Valiant efforts were made to find cooperative ways to meet this challenge; many such programs are described in the September 1965 issue of the *ALA Bulletin*.[4] However, the situation reached a national crisis stage in the early 1960's. Alarm over this "student problem" brought some 4,000 librarians together to discuss possible "cures" at the 1963 ALA Conference-within-a-Conference (CWC) in Chicago.[5]

Certainly that conference serves as a landmark which influenced many participants to follow a variety of action patterns. For example, committees were established at local and/or state levels for considering ways to meet the needs of both the students and the total population. From such committees came statements defining the roles of the various types of libraries, setting policy for action, or giving direction to teachers and students concerning use of the various library facilities.

Since the 1963 CWC, other ALA meetings have directly or indirectly attempted to move forward in this area. The ALA Young Adult Services Division's 1966 Pre-Conference in Library Programs for Disadvantaged Youth gave evidence of successful action programs; examples included the one in Nassau where the public library made yearly loans of "study kits" to disadvantaged students and "Detroit Adventure," where young adult librarians gave leadership for book discussions in classrooms in conjunction with high school English departments.[6] Again, in Kansas City in the summer of 1968, a day's program was jointly sponsored by CSD, American Association of School Librarians, Public Librarians Association and Young Adult Service Division in order to consider how they could best cooperate.

It is too soon to cite examples of possible effects from the latter deliberations. It is true that we tend to feel impatient with the amount of talking we do about these questions and perhaps think that nothing much happens. However, in checking the literature in preparation for this meeting I found a substantial amount of activity in the five years since the 1963 conference. Some of it relating to the meetings held at that conference.

Perhaps less directly affecting interlibrary cooperation where schools are involved is the Knapp School Library Project. The final report[7] on this indicates that at least in some of the situations the program had a yeasty effect in making the community aware of needs and of involvement of the cooperating teacher education institution with the question of supply and use of materials as well as preparation of teachers for effective use of libraries.

Finally, but not least important, has been the impact made by federal funds. First, the Library Services and Construction Act and the State Library Development Committees provided much statewide planning. The amount of concern about the school age user has varied from state to state. Presently, with Library Services and Construction Act Titles III and IV being implemented, there is more direct involvement. The National Defence Education Act Title III, and the Elementary and Secondary Education Act Title II funds have helped build school library collections and this very fact has promoted a healthy climate for cooperation. If nothing else, in a few cases the availability of the federal funds has brought together people from separate fields to do some joint planning.

James Cass observed in the *Saturday Review* that, "Education reporting today is very much like snapping a photo of a moving object—by the time the shutter has clicked, the picture has changed."[8] In a sense, this is also true of the library situation. It is especially difficult to find good reports on what has actually happened; often there are references to studies in progress, but it is sometimes impossible to locate final results. Before or by the tenth anniversary of the Conference-within-a-Conference it would be desirable to have reached another landmark, some type of nation-wide evaluation of the various cooperative ventures in which we are now engaged. Returning to the subject of state-level policy statements, three might be cited as being especially helpful; they come from Oregon, Washington and Wisconsin. The concluding paragraph of the Wisconsin statement summarizes the major emphasis of most such statements: "While every avenue will be explored to promote cooperation and coordination of school and public libraries, their functions are clearly distinct, and neither library is capable of providing or should attempt to provide the services of the other."[9]

To expand the concepts on which such a statement is based, I would like to quote at length from a source other than a policy statement devised in any one state. It is by Violet Wagener of the Boulder Valley School District in Colorado. It seems the best description of what we all need to understand and appreciate about the functions of school and public libraries.

School and public libraries are educational institutions which have been serving as learning motivators and independent learning centers. The much younger school library was formed to provide a readily accessible and diversified collection of books and periodicals to supplement textbooks and enrich curricula. Audio-visual materials were added when there was recognition of the importance of sensory stimuli for learning, that certain content is learned more readily in nonprint form, and when it was suspected that students have individual learning styles.

The school library then became an instructional materials center, remaining materials oriented instead of program or learner oriented, and providing a balanced instead of a specialized collection. Now the school library is evolving into an information and communication center, a learning center, resource center, or an entire self-contained school, program oriented with materials collection for curricular concepts, behavioral objectives and instructional modes, and specially coded for teacher access to individualize instruction.

The differences between the school library and public library as institutions for motivating learning and providing materials for independent learning are becoming more pronounced. The school is the developer and guide of the inquiry process for learning. It motivates and manipulates the learning environment so that, hopefully, each student will learn how to learn and be inspired to continue to learn the remainder of his life. He should acquire from his school experience fundamental knowledge, concepts, and basic physical, psycho-motor and intellectual skills to enable him to function as an independent learner. The public library is the storehouse and resource for this independent learner, young or old. The school library must provide resources for professional needs of educators and a wide variety of resources to meet the prescribed instructional needs of students with intellectual, experimental and psychological differences. The school library must also serve as an information and communication link with the public library and other community agencies for the independent school age learner.

The public library is particularly effective as a learning motivator for the preschool age child, as a resource for the school age child who is an independent learner, for parent-child initiated learning, for adults who are independent learners, and as a generalized information center. It should be able to refer to the school library requests for education information and be able to utilize school developed prescribed learning programs requested by adult patrons. The school library should be able to refer students on independent learning projects to the public library, or obtain generalized reference information assistance from it for teachers and students. These dynamic evolving relationships of the school library within the school and the school library with the public library require flexible people developing flexible plans for flexible institutions. Proper selection of materials and analysis of proper location of materials for economy and efficiency of learning and funds must be worked out within each local community but within the context of the education role of both school and public libraries. An allowance must also be made for the larger community of needs and resources brought closer daily through systems development and electronic devices.[10]

To summarize, the development of any service or system should accommodate concurrently developing systems and should be compatible with larger networks.

Because so many places have used a specific basic document in formulating policy, it is appropriate to quote from the most pertinent section of the 1961 publication of the Council of Chief State School Officers, *Responsibilities of State Departments of Education for School Library Services:*

a. The school library serves the school, and the public library serves the community. Teachers and pupils are members of both the school and the community.

b. Public library service—including service from state, regional, county, and community libraries—may supplement but never supplant the school library. Service which replaces the school library impedes the development of school libraries to the detriment of service to teachers and pupils and tends to separate library materials from instructional programs.

c. The school has the primary responsibility for instruction and guidance of children and youth in the community in the use of libraries. The program of library instruction, directed by the school librarians, has the broad purposes of teaching library skills adaptable to all types of libraries and for encouraging pupils to use libraries for continuing self-education. School librarians, teachers, and public librarians should cooperate in planning instructional programs in the use of libraries for educational programs in the use of libraries for educational and recreational purposes.

d. Cooperative planning in the selection and utilization of materials for children and young people is the responsibility of school administrators, teachers, school librarians, public librarians, and other community leaders concerned with youth.

These principles apply in urban and rural communities and to both elementary and secondary schools. In urban and other nonrural communities the recent tremendous increase in the number of students using the resources of community libraries has pointed to the need for cooperative planning by school, college, and public library administrators concerning library services to students within the same geographic areas. In rural communities some school boards and administrators are moving toward the development of strong reorganized school districts able to provide good school libraries, while others are beginning to provide school library service from intermediate units.

State library extension agencies, primarily concerned with public libraries, have gradually withdrawn direct service to schools as their programs have matured and as boards of education have become able to support and administer school libraries. In some states with undeveloped school library programs direct service from State library extension agencies to schools still exists. However, in these states the principles of school and public library relations should be applied as soon as possible, and the full responsibility for State-level services to school libraries should be assumed by State departments of education.[11]

In addition to the landmarks of LSCA, ESEA, the Conference-within-a-Conference, and so forth, we would be remiss if we did not mention the importance to cooperative planning of the new standards published for both public and school libraries at a time when such basic tools were most important.

While it is important to know of the over-all national trends and developments, it may be more helpful to have specific examples from some of the states. Of the ones whose cooperative activities I was able to study, perhaps New Jersey is most interesting and relevant. This state's developmental program dates back ten years when major emphasis was on public libraries. And, of course, New Jersey is not alone in discovering that it does not work to upgrade only the one type of library. Thus a survey was begun in 1962-63, which focused on the needs of readers, not on the libraries as institutions. Equally important was the broad base of involvement of librarians who served as members of many subcommitties working with the Library Development Committee on the survey. The Committee was composed of representatives of public, school, special, college, and university librarians, as well as trustees and people from other lay interests.

Focusing on the reader, New Jersey found that library categories and political jurisdictions mean nothing to the person who wants to use the most convenient or the best source. The Committee working with the survey results developed a plan with several phases: minimum standards were set first for: local public libraries, elementary libraries (K-6), secondary libraries (7-12), and four-year college libraries.

Their second level activity, for which LSCA Title I funds were used, was to begin establishing area libraries to serve as back-up collections for all types of libraries. Area libraries are open to all residents of the area with reference and reading guidance services available to them; area libraries also provide to public, school and college libraries interlibrary information and reference services. This phase of the plan is only partially in operation while third level goals are still to be implemented.

I believe this plan is worthy of detailed study; for one thing, New Jersey and Illinois have certain similarities in having the extremes of urbanization and rural conditions existing side by side. In the second place, development has progressed to the point where it is easy to see where difficulties will arise. The survey report written by Martin, Gaver and Monroe[12] and material on the status of the plan's implementation as of 1967 are also of interest.

As Bryan noted at the tenth annual Syracuse Symposium:

To summarize how the plan works, it is now expected that any individual with a serious intention and need can have his requirements met through a chain of library opportunity that starts at the school, passes through the local public library and the area reference library to any or all four research libraries and the reference referral office of the State Library, which will search outside of the state for needed information or materials should circumstances require. In addition, however, the very fact that each area reference library is required by regulation of the state agency to have a coordinating committee of librarians. . .means that there is not only overview of the operation of the system but also regular evaluation and report.[13]

He emphasizes in addition, that since the area libraries and the research libraries accept funds for these services they are now obliged to provide them. While the New Jersey plan is not fully implemented it would so far seem that advantages outweigh disadvantages and that "the public" is generally in favor of it. Before returning to the discussion of some of the activities in Hawaii, I will mention some other typical programs. In Oklahoma, for instance, a committee appointed by the governor was made up of five librarians and four lay people. It conducted a survey and planned a governor's conference on libraries; two state school library supervisors were secured for the Department of Education. In the survey, it was found that many resources are available in academic libraries but little thought has been given to using them for service to students in the state as a whole. Such a large state as New York has a person who works out of the Library Development Division as a liaison with the Bureau of School Library Service. They still lack an over-all development program to meet the needs of elementary, high school and early college level students. Recent studies by Nelson Associates recommend experimentation with joint facilities for school and public libraries in small localities—a recommendation of interest to us in Hawaii since we also are experimenting in this area. The studies also recommend that school libraries be placed as a third bureau under the Library Development Division (now consisting of public libraries, and academic and research libraries).[14]

One other type of involvement, developing informational publications at the state level is represented by South Carolina's publication, "Tips for Teachers." This is specifically on the assignment problem and was produced by the State Library Board.

Wisconsin's policy summary statement was quoted earlier. Wisconsin carries on a program which is found in some other states also; their Cooperative Children's Book Center is located in the State Capital, is under the direction of the children's consultant on the State Library staff, is co-sponsored by the Department of Public Instruction and the University of Wisconsin, and paid for from LSCA funds. This is a special non-circulating collection of children's books and selected audio-visual materials for examination, reading, evaluation, study and use by on-the-job librarians, students and can be evaluated by the teachers and ordered for their school libraries.

One of the most ambitious projects involved the states of Utah, Colorado and Wyoming and involved 30,000 children from 120 schools and public libraries in a reading program.

These then are a few examples of some of the activities going on in certain representative states. Since Hawaii represents as close an administrative tie as would be possible for school and public and state library services, I will discuss some of the things which have been done there. Some of the programs were well underway before there was an actual organizational bond. Some grew directly from recommendations made by Robert Leigh in 1960, when he made the first of various studies which followed statehood; he indicated it would be better for the library system to be within the Department of Education, providing the state librarian would have the status of an assistant superintendent.

First then, let us look at his recommendations made almost ten years ago, on the relation of public and school libraries:

> *Recommended* that as general policy and plan, school libraries and public library branches be built and maintained in separate quarters under separate management, but with close working relations through joint planning and acquisitions committees in each of the counties.[15]

Of some forty school libraries and a dozen or more public libraries built since that time only three have not followed this recommendation. We have just started a two-year depth study of the services being given by these three joint operations, all of which are in small, rural communities.

> *Recommended* that the Public Libraries Division and the Director of (School) Library Services, in the Department of Education, plan jointly for, and schedule the transfer of public library bookmobile and other emergency public library services to the schools without libraries, to the school libraries as they are developed.[15]

New standards for bookmobile services were adopted; stops at schools are after-school stops, serving as community stops, unless there is an emergency situation. This situation compares favorably to the former bookmobile program built around school stops.

> *Recommended* that the Public Libraries Division and the Director of (School) Libraries establish in each of the four counties under the joint leadership of the County Librarian and District School Superintendent a permanent, working committee on book acquisition for school and public libraries, to work out formulas for book acquisition for the school ages in the two types of libraries, also to deal with the problem of relating teaching assignments to readily available library resources.[15]

Joint committees for school-public library relations were set up in each county, based on this recommendation. One of these committees continues to meet feeling that it is a helpful activity. However, the major objective is fulfilled by the establishment of a book evaluation group on a statewide basis. From each geographical district one elementary and one secondary school librarian is brought to Honolulu for a monthly meeting. All children and young adult librarians attend the all-day sessions when work is done on the lists from which all libraries order current titles. A total of fifty to seventy school librarians participate in reviewing new titles. In addition, others work on a continuing evaluation of our so-called replacement lists. While this particular cooperative activity was well underway before the state library system absorbed the School Libraries and Instructional Materials Branch, having the joint administrative set-up does make the program easier to operate. The district superintendents select the school librarins who will be involved and we try to keep a balance between those who have been on the committee and those who are new.

*Suggested* that if an accidentally favorable geographical situation presents itself in a Honolulu urban area or in a sparsely populated rural area, or in both areas, at the time of planning a new school building and a public library branch, (a) the Department of Education *experiment* with the combination of a public library branch with a specially trained school and children's and young peoples' librarian in charge of a school library section, the branch to be contiguous to, or attached to, the school building, (b) that an outside, objective agency be engaged at the outset to conduct a field study to determine the comparative advantages and disadvantages of the combined library in service to the adults in the area, to students and faculty in the school, and to students coming from other schools to use the combined library, the results of the study to help determine in what other situations, if any, a combined library might be practicable.[15]

As noted earlier there have been community-school libraries opened in three locations since 1962. Just now the first one really designed for full service is being opened with a staff of ten to take care of the diverse needs of the two types of users. This library provides a local production center for the school and community and its humanities room will serve as a small auditorium, for closed circuit television, art displays, and so on.

*Recommended:* (a) that each of the four county public libraries develop fully and maintain a special collection of professional books and other materials for reading and reference by teachers, by school officers as well as by interested parents and citizens; these collections to be in addition to reports, manuals and curricular programs being used currently in the schools which are properly located in each of the school libraries; (b) that the Public Libraries Division assign to the Library of Hawaii or another cooperating library the task of preparing and distributing periodically to the other interested libraries an annotated list and buying guide for new educational publications.[15]

Since 1965 special allotments have been made so that each district office is building up a professional collection. The concept of the district office has changed somewhat since Leigh's report was made and the location of the collections in those offices is preferred. The buying guide for professional materials is prepared by the School Libraries Section annually in cooperation with the librarian for the education collection at the State Library and the subject specialists in the state department of education. This list is used by schools also and each school receives some special funds to use for professional materials. This particular project received special legislature appropriation and took care of a great need.

*Suggested* that the Oahu School District film collection or the Library of Hawaii Film Service be made available to the schools of all the Islands on equal terms, or that the two collections be combined and operated as a school and adult film service by the Library of Hawaii.[15]

The two film collections continue to be administered separately, primarily due to a legal question relating to service to private schools. Following an U.S. Office of Education survey of audio-visual services in Hawaii soon after Leigh's study was made, these steps were taken:

1) Distribution of 16 m.m. films was extended to all districts rather than to only those on Oahu;

2) Other types of services were discontinued such as filmstrips, recordings and study prints;

3) Consultative service was stepped up;

4) A position was added and both school libraries and audio-visual services were placed under the same director;

5) Small collections of most frequently used films were placed in the district offices on each of the three neighbor islands;

6) A major expansion has been in the area of audio tape duplication during the past two years. From several thousand master tapes, with high speed equipment both public and school library needs are being met; and

7) Films are sent by mail (air lifted) to the other islands while another joint program takes care of Oahu deliveries; once a week films are delivered to Oahu public library branches where they picked up by school personnel.

Suggested that a continuing intra-departmental committee or other method of regular communication, be established in the Department of Education, representing the Adult Education Unit and the Public Libraries Division, with the purpose of joint planning and of securing full cooperation of the public libraries, their facilities and collections, in programs of adult education developed by the Adult Education Unit.[15]

A librarian serves on the Adult Education Advisory Committee. While efforts in this area are not as structured as Leigh envisioned, a great deal is done as various opportunities arise in specific agencies. For example, the Basic Education for Adult Illiterates Programs have used the branch libraries extensively for study.

There are a number of on-going programs which require cooperation of several agencies above and beyond those described above as related to Leigh's recommendations. One of the most stimulating, the Nene award, involves the two branches within our library system and also private schools and the professional associations. The Nene, or native goose, is the state bird and was selected as a symbol for reading promotion. Initiated some years ago, the award is designed to be of interest to children in upper elementary grandes. Selection is for a work of a living author and nominations are made in the spring. During the summer, schools loan their copies of Nene "nominees" to neighbor public libraries when needed and children are urged to read them so they know as many as possible. Some counties have had additional cooperative summer reading programs. This has been an effective device for getting librarians together on an interesting project as well as in getting children to read. Authors who have won the award include Scott O'Dell, Pamela Travers and Beverly Cleary. O'Dell is the only one who has been able to visit Hawaii after receiving it. The school making the original "nomination" has possession for a year of the large wooden plaque depicting the Nene.

On the secondary level we have an equally stimulating project which involves over 3,500 students in public and private schools, a number of social studies teachers, school and public librarians as well as the consultant staff in the state library system. Each year the Pacific and Asian Affairs Council (PAAC) sponsors a discussion program for students and we (Young Adult Section and School Libraries Section) do the bibliographies for them as well as supplying copies of the materials to public libraries. This year the theme is "Man's Search for a World Without War" while last year's was "Winds of Change—World in Revolution." The lists are very important since in a certain sense they both reflect and guide the development of the topics. There is an added tie-in with the East-West Center at the University of Hawaii.

Spanning all levels, we have for a number of years been involved with the University preparation of the quarterly "Current Hawaiian," a list, which then goes to all school libraries.

A number of interesting joint ventures started last year and among other things involved the testing of various pieces of equipment in schools under the auspices of the State Library. In one case, for example, we were concerned with teaching functionally illiterate children who have high learning potential. From the school comes diagnostic procedures, personnel and equipment which are available in any secondary school; while the State Library provides some additional equipment, in this case a modification of language laboratory equipment. The office of School Libraries and Instructional Materials provided duplication of tapes after the Library for the Blind volunteers did master tapes. Large print books were supplied from a special collection administered by the State Library Branch. This basically accomplished the adoption of methods used for individual instruction to group instruction. The equipment was located in the school library. The project proposal charged the Office of Library Services with evaluating for both public and school libraries the result and implications that this program could have for other programs.

Following this evaluation the plan is to extend the program to the students of the correctional institution; these students are in many cases functional illiterates and can now be certified to use the materials from the Library for the Blind.

We have initiated the use of materials for adults which have long been associated with the classroom; these include flash cards and labels, the tachistoscope, transparencies and audio-tapes. At the present time plans made last year are in the implementation stage; these include development of a joint program under LSCA for two of our state schools for handicapped children.

Probably of greatest interest is the question of how Hawaii's Central Processing Center provides service for state, school and public libraries. While this is our newest "branch," the recent feasibility study made by Boaz, Allen and Hamilton would place the operation in a new administrative and technical services branch. Other changes are recommended in this weighty document but those which relate to areas affecting cooperative activities are not in operation as yet nor are we sure of schedules for implementation.

Looking forward to further changes because of this latest study, I can appreciate hesitancy any librarians may feel as they attempt to build a state plan. However, in looking back over the tremendous changes already made in Hawaii, I can close with some specific suggestions: as a school person most recently, but with experience in public libraries with both children and young people, I believe that the greatest need in "division of labors" is for the public libraries to put great emphasis on the pre-school program and on programs for teenagers which will somehow speak to their needs and interests. I would recommend highly the article in *American Education*[16] on the liaison librarians because it gives guidance in the way one may move at both state and local levels in work with young adults and teenagers.

As you develop plans and then programs, do accentuate the positive. Try to think of individuals who should be involved at the planning stage and see that they are included. Plans should not be too grandiose; plan a series of steps toward a final goal so that the small successes will be apparent and encouraging.

## References

1. Hawaii. Department of Education. Office of Library Services. *Planning for Libraries in Hawaii, a Comprehensive Statewide Planning and Feasibility Study for Public Libraries and Joint School and Public Library Facilities.* 1968, p. 23.

2. Batchelder, Mildred L. "Public Library Influence on School Libraries," *Library Trends,* 1:271-285, Jan. 1953.

3. Rathbone, Josephine A. "Cooperation between Libraries and Schools: An Historical Sketch," *Library Journal,* 26:187-191, Apr. 1901.

4. Yungmeyer, Elinor, ed. "Cooperation in Action," *ALA Bulletin,* 59:733-744, Sept. 1965.

5. American Library Association. *Student Use of Libraries, An Inquiry into the Needs of Students, Libraries, and the Educational Process.* Chicago, ALA, 1964.

6. American Library Association. Young Adult Services Division. *Preconference: Two Blocks Apart.* July 8-10, 1965. (Kit for participants.)

7. Sullivan, Peggy, ed. *Realization: the Final Report of the Knapp School Libraries Project.* Chicago, ALA, 1968.

8. Cass, James. "Where the Action is," *Saturday Review,* 49:69, Oct. 15, 1966.

9. Wisconsin. Department of Public Instruction. "Public Library and School Library: Organizational Relationships; a Policy Statement," *Wisconsin Library Bulletin,* 63:94, Mar.-Apr. 1967.

10. Wagener, Violet. "Title III Resources Center Begins Operation," *The Capitol Hill Library Crier* (Colorado State Library), 9:16-17, May 1968.

11. Council of Chief State School Officers. *Responsibilities of State Departments of Education for School Library Services.* Washington, D.C., The Council, 1961, pp. 14-16.

12. New Jersey Library Association Library Development Committee. *Libraries for the People of New Jersey, or Knowledge for all.* New Brunswick, N.J., The Committee, 1964.

13. Bryan, James E. "Cooperation in New Jersey." *In* Dorothy A. McGinniss, ed., *Libraries and Youth: Cooperation to give Service to Children and Young People.* School of Library Science, Syracuse University, 1968, pp. 27-28.

14. New York (State) Division of Evaluation. *Emerging Library Systems.* Albany, University of the State of New York, 1967, pp. 84-85.

15. Leigh, Robert D. *Governor's Study of Public and School Libraries in the State of Hawaii.* Vol. 1. Honolulu, Hawaii Dept. of Public Instruction, 1960, pp. 77-78.

16. Winnick, Pauline and Horn, W. A. "The Liaison Librarian," *American Education,* 4:26-27, Dec. 1967-Jan. 1968.

Russell Shank
*Director of Libraries*
*Smithsonian Institution*
*Washington, D.C.*

# COOPERATION BETWEEN SPECIAL LIBRARIES AND OTHER TYPES OF LIBRARIES

The student of special libraries struggles first with defining them. Special libraries exist in every environment, hence if I define them too broadly, there is no group other than themselves with which they may interact. However, it is obvious that for systems planning purposes, whatever we do about academic and public libraries benefits branches within them that are considered under some definitions to be special libraries. Therefore, I have set these on the "other" side, and have defined the special libraries on which this essay will focus to be those that exist in business, industry, government, museums, societies, and non-profit research agencies. It is in this group that we find several types which are constrained by their parent organizations from responding to normal techniques of promoting cooperative activities, and for examination their isolation should prove useful.

Special libraries form two subsets when analyzed in terms of interagency cooperation, particularly with academic and public libraries. The special libraries in government, museums, societies and non-profit agencies form one subset, those in business and industry another. While none of these libraries has a public responsibility as its primary mission, the former are more frequently considered, and behave more like quasi-public libraries. The latter do not, and can easily draw away from any association with or contribution to the public sector of library service. In other words, the former group may well be considered for planning purposes to be the open sector of special libraries, the latter should be dealt with as the closed sector. The libraries of the industrial and business group are generally categorized as users by the open sector and not generally as partners in public systems.

This situation need not necessarily be perpetuated. The special, closed characteristic of the corporate library has meaning, nevertheless, in terms of

60

what must be done to capitalize on any semblance of accessibility that the special library in the profit-making sector displays. As many as half of the non-academic and non-public special libraries are in business and industry. This group constitutes a number too large to bypass in systems planning.

In essaying the field of special libraries we are hampered by an annoying dearth of good, sound, research information, including statistical data, relating to almost every aspect of work with these libraries. It is indeed strange that a field of librarianship so prominent, and with both serious problems and examples of excellent solutions to these problems, has itself been so little studied. Most of the literature about special librarianship is descriptive of techniques or argumentative about philosophy. Three theses dealing with various aspects of business and industrial special libraries, and their inter-relationships, a score of state and regional planning documents, the documentation concerning fewer than half-a-dozen on-going service systems, and many articles on the problems and operations of special libraries and services that feed them provided input for this essay. My own work over two decades in special research libraries, and particularly my work for the New York City 3-R's agency in its efforts to increase access to scientific and technical information, strongly influenced my analysis of the relationships between special and other libraries.

In many respects what I have seen and have to say may not be unique to the relationships between special and other types of libraries. Many of the problems that affect system development in libraries are universal. This was one of the outstanding characteristics of my findings in a New York City study that pointedly and intensely concentrated on a type of library considered "special." We must consider this fortunate, since many of our proposed solutions to problems of extending library service in general will easily encompass and benefit special libraries. Nevertheless, the special library environment does harbor some peculiarities that are unique, or at least different enough from the norm of public and academic libraries to require exceptional features in systems designed to enhance the power of libraries through cooperation or formalized interaction.

Quite naturally the largest part of the interaction among special libraries and between special and other types of libraries still comes about through informal or non-systematized contacts, with the libraries operating quite independently and under no obligation to participate in the transactions. The chief output of interaction is the sharing of resources through interlibrary lending. Interlibrary cooperation in reference services, except for the normal interchange of courtesies in answering quick reference questions by phone and mail, is minimal.

Only the scantiest of recent evidence can be presented to demonstrate the patterns and the dimensions of the interlibrary lending activity. In a New York State study, corporate special libraries reported that they sought publications from various sources in the following order of preference: other special libraries, federal government agency libraries, college and public libraries (showing no difference in order of preference), research centers, other out-of-state libraries, experts, and the New York State Library.[1]

One fourth of the special libraries used other special libraries most frequently; between 15 and 18 percent used federal government, public and the state libraries most frequently; and about 11 percent used college libraries most frequently. The median number of items received on interlibrary transactions was 100. Books comprised 30 percent of the total items borrowed, 27 percent were photocopies in lieu of interlibrary loan, and 22 percent were serials. Dan Bedsole found that on a nationwide basis, the average number of volumes borrowed by industrial corporation libraries was about 335 per year, with a high of 10,000 reported by one library. This same group of special libraries contributed about fifty-seven volumes a year to the interlibrary lending operation and although the point is not made, we may presume from other experience that most of those volumes were lent to other special libraries. The remainder of the volumes in the interlibrary loan pipeline studied by Bedsole represent a load factor of about 650,000 volumes a year flowing from various sources other than special libraries to the nation's 2,400 industrial libraries.[2]

The New York City survey of science library facilities and services calculated that four of the largest public science collections in the city were being tapped for 30,000 photocopy requests a year for journal articles, or about 200 text pages per hour, with as much as 90 percent of the load coming from industry.[3] All three of these pieces of evidence indicate that the workload in interlibrary activity is large enough to invite planned accommodation. Although this is skimpy evidence with which to encourage widespread planning, the fact that three studies with different purposes found interlibrary sharing of resources to be big business is not coincidental. The need for planning is real.

The tendency for special libraries to cooperate with libraries of similar kinds is strong.[4] This is particularly true of medical and law libraries, undoubtedly because of the special features and contents of their literature bases that are used by no one outside of these disciplines. To the extent that libraries in these subject areas exist within organizations of different types (e.g., academic, hospital, county, association and industrial corporations), cooperation among the libraries is a demonstration of how agencies with disparate goals and support can interface in a system. Medical libraries are being even more closely bound into a stratified cooperative structure by the policies and practices of the National Library of Medicine (NLM) in disseminating literature and citations to doctors through libraries, and the strengthening of the structure through the provisions of the Medical Library Assistance Act which places a premium on cooperation.[5] NLM itself is purposefully planning a hierarchy of libraries and information centers in the extension of MEDLARS.[6]

Museum libraries and academic libraries appear to have a natural affinity, chiefly because the museum curator conducts research much in the same fashion as a professor, and indeed in a number of fields, such as systematic biology and art history, professors and curators are peers, sharing research resources, joint appointments and professional society affiliations. Except for an attempt to create an automated inventory of some parts of a number of museums' artifacts through the aegis of the Museum Computer Network in New York City, nothing is yet developing that would tie together museum libraries with those of academies of science, universities, societies and foundations, all of which share many other characteristics in common with museums.[7] This situation might change if the National Museum Act can be extended and funded.[8]

Few societies maintain libraries in the United States, but those that do have, in the main, superb research facilities. Although they exist primarily to serve members, they are most often open for public use on the premises. The Chemists' Club Library in New York City is entirely non-circulating even to members, hence any interaction that takes place is through the medium of the users from various kinds of agencies who come to the library. On the other hand, the Engineering Societies Library (ESL) does lend books to members, and has established a class of membership for corporate libraries which then are entitled to borrow materials just as the members of the societies that support ESL.

Unsystematic interlibrary activity is not sufficient to the task of supplying information and publications in the breadth of subjects and depth of analysis that is demanded by our highly developed intellectual communities of users. The "unsystem" can respond neither quickly nor cheaply enough, even though several recent studies seem to indicate otherwise. Several studies note that special libraries are filling nearly 100 percent of all requests made of them with considerable reliance on other libraries.[9] This is taken by some to indicate a lack of need to improve services. Yet this evidence of satisfaction obscures difficulties that demand attention.

In the unstructured system of libraries with which he operates, the special librarian must often hunt through a sequence of many libraries before finding material he needs and to which he can have access. This is costly and time-consuming communication. Furthermore, even though public and academic libraries may rank third or fourth on the list of most frequently used sources by special libraries, the burden on these libraries has reached the cirsis point in most places. Special library users are demanding. After making the rounds of other kinds of libraries all that may remain of their needs when they come to the pbulic sector are the items most difficult to identify and locate, the obscure, or the heavily used material that no one else can find or will lend them. Regardless of the number of libraries in a region, the biggest part of the burden of interlibrary lending usually falls on one or a few large libraries. Thus, among science libraries in the New York City area, four libraries (New York Public Library, ESL, Columbia University and the Chemists' Club) are the most frequently visited, the most frequently called, the most frequently tapped for photocopies, and the most frequently criticized libraries of the scores of units in the public sector.

These are the forces that have influenced the building of systems and networks among libraries. The goal is always the same: to expand the vista of the libraries and their users to take into account more of the region's resources, to increase the probability of success in searching for material, or to decrease the probability of following false leads, and to simplify and speed up communication of information and publications. In a few instances, the goals are expanded to include the increase of the region's resources in a response patterned after need, and the establishment of new public services.

Organizational structures, services, and system facilities vary among the regions in which cooperation has been formalized as would be expected given the variation in influences in various regions and metropolitan areas. The publication by local libraries of lists with their collections specialties, accessibility to the public and service offerings is a minimum, and frequently invoked, technique of systematization. A list of special libraries of all kinds has been available in New York City for decades.[10] A similar but smaller list is the only real product of the Associated Science Libraries of San Diego, a group of industrial, academic, government, and museum libraries.[11]

Stronger links—usually involving positive commitments by several libraries to serve as the core of a system and as some kind of dedicated communication circuit—have been created or are being recommended by planners who hope these links will be innovative and instrumental in initiating continued developments and refinements. Again patterns of operation vary, and we have no analysis of the reasons for, or the comparative success of, the various patterns. In Dallas the pool of resources of the Industrial Information Service, established to serve business and industry, has been created by the holdings of a number of academic libraries backed up by the holdings of Southern Methodist University where the service is located.[12] The same is true in Houston for the Regional Information and Communication Exchange headquartered at Rice University.[13] Users in Dallas including corporate libraries tap the system through the headquarters office of the Industrial Information Service. In the Gulf area, members of RICE, and others in business and industry, tap the system wherever a core library is located. The core libraries in both systems are linked by teletype. A proposed plan for Connecticut would link pre-identified libraries together with teletype, but would tie the network to a statewide library research center where an automated union catalog would be maintained.[14] Participating libraries, among which are eighteen corporate and many academic libraries, would insert cataloging copy in machine-readable form as their collections grew. Presumably other libraries could query the system, perhaps for a fee.

In New York City, the establishment of a system of core libraries to serve as a public resource in science and technology, including public, government, society, academic, association, and museum libraries where strong collections in various subjects are already maintained has been proposed.[15] The subjects covered by the collections are complementary, with some redundancy. Users would access the system in normal ways, and through network communication facilities yet to be developed, would be given a number of physical access points to the entire system.

But of even greater importance, the core libraries would be subsidized so that the growth of the collections in specified subject areas which serve the public interest would be guaranteed and not left to the unilateral decisions of libraries operating independently. Furthermore, the subsidy would compensate the libraries for the adoption of a public function that might lie somewhere beyond its normal responsibility, thereby protecting its own resources which are to be directed to its basic missions and clientele.

I have already mentioned the hierarchies of libraries being developed into an inter-agency system by the National Library of Medicine. The mixture of medical libraries one finds in various regions have been the most active in creating a new environment for library service. In New York City most of the hospital, academic, research and institutional medical libraries operate a cooperative storage and delivery system and maintain a union list of serials.[16]

Several regional groupings of libraries based on units of the State University of New York are demonstrating network capabilities for locating and sharing resources.[17] In Detroit a group of nine academic and institutional medical libraries have formed a strong federation with their technical services being performed by Wayne State University.[18] Wayne State has long been the chief contributor to interlibrary loans among medical libraries, and continues to be the depth resource. This system operates within a larger, but more loosely knit, group of nearly thirty medical libraries, including academic, institutional and industrial libraries, that have for years been researching problems of mutual concern in medical library operation, and have contributed to a union list of serials that Wayne State produces for the group.

At this point let me turn away from the cataloging of cooperative ventures, for obviously there are many. In many instances they are the reverse images of some of the cooperative programs that have already been mentioned. Let us now examine some of the factors which influence the planning improvements in the quality of experiences in contacts between special and other kinds of libraries.

The aspect of "specialness" of these libraries that ultimately brings to bear the strongest influences on making plans for their incorporation into viable systems and networks derives from the mission of their parent agencies. Subject content and kind of materials in the collections of special libraries are important considerations in systems planning, as are the geographical location of special libraries and their information and service orientation. Nevertheless in the final analysis it is not these elements but those that are determined by whether the agency that pays for the special library is profit or non-profit, is in research, manufacturing, education or business, that determines what alternatives we must select in building a conglomorate system of libraries of varying types. System design is severely constrained, therefore, by influences determined by the nature of the agency and not necessarily by its information and library needs and its resources.

One of the most difficult administrative problems of providing for interaction between special and other types of libraries is the financing of such operations. Corporate libraries as a category are frequently excluded from programs that are funded by the state since it is not usually state policy to subsidize, at least directly, industrial corporations for what are considered normal operations. In New York State, funds distributed by the State Library to the 3-R's regional agencies may go only to incorporated non-profit cultural or educatonal institutions (including public libraries) which provide reference and research library service. Funds cannot be further distributed to profit-making agencies.[19] It is not even clear yet whether corporate libraries can participate in special programs to aid libraries that are funded with 3-R's money. A "corporate" library membership category has recently been established by the New York City 3-R's agency (METRO). These libraries will receive at least their pro-rata share of service upon the payment of dues, if not the full services from METRO.

Special libraries benefit from government-subsidized programs that tend to improve public and academic libraries, and indeed, a number of programs of this type have been funded that have been of immediate importance to corporate libraries. For several years, the National Science Foundation and the Department of Commerce joined forces to finance a dozen regional technical report centers, mostly in universities throughout the country (except in Illinois where the John Crerar Library was the depository).[20] The Department of Commerce provided microfilm copies of technical reports from its Clearinghouse for Federal Scientific and Technical Information and the National Science Foundation paid for staff and equipment to manage the centers' operations. The idea, of course, was to improve access to technical reports, a service of vital importance to many industrial libraries among others. State Technical Services Act funds have provided seed money for the Regional Information and Communication Exchange in Houston, the Industrial Information Service in Dallas, and a program in California that links the State Library, UCLA, and public libraries in the Fresno County area—all to serve industry.[21]

Surprisingly, in spite of much talk among academic and public libraries, few of them charge corporate users for their services. Stanford and M.I.T. have established technical information service divisions or departments to which local corporate agencies pay fees for service, and some libraries such as the University of California at Berkeley have user's or borrower's fees, although these are usually quite nominal[22] -as are the services offered. There is still a strong feeling among many such libraries that corporations are entitled to access to publicly supported libraries (including those in academic institutions) as their right for having paid their taxes. Robert Muller has rather succinctly disposed of this argument and other basic premises under which free services are offered to industry. Basically, his point is that corporate libraries and their users are entitled to, and do receive, whatever level of library service can be offered for the funds appropriated for public and academic libraries. Corporate libraries need more specialized services, however than can be justified for the public good. On this point Muller says:

> If the public interest requires that service be given to all those needing it, a governmental agency is likely to be set up, and subsidization can be justified. On the other hand, where service does not clearly relate to the public interest, justification is needed if service is supplied below cost or free. A publicly supported institution is even more subject to criticism than a privately supported one when it gives things away. The "thing" given away by a university library is often not conspicuously visible, but is just as real: It is staff time paid for by appropriated funds that might have been better spent on service to students and faculty.[23]

The Engineering Societies Library and the John Crerar Library both offer special services such as compilation of bibliographies and the provision of translations, priced at cost. Perhaps all libraries with attractive resources such as these should be more mercenary in dealing with those who need exceptional services. The federal government very pointedly recognizes the value of information in its various technology transfer programs. According to one recent analysis by NASA:

> Technical information is a marketable commodity. True transfer programs add value to that information by abstracting, categorizing,

separating out the significant, dividing the relevant from the non-relevant, and by interpretation, analysis, repackaging, and provision of local access. The user of a system should therefore be expected to share in the cost of its operation.[24]

Lest you get too optimistic that we have found the key to the coffers, let me warn you that there are some limits. For example, the experience of those libraries and information centers that sell bibliographic search services indicates that users, including corporations, are willing under normal circumstances to buy searches for which the cost is not more than a few hundred dollars. The average cost of a search at the Engineering Societies Library in a recent year was $124. On the other hand, at least one corporation pays up to $1,000 a month for a special service from one of these libraries for which it receives filmed copies of articles and punched cards for processing and announcement services within the company.[25] Furthermore, services for sale must be pertinent, of high quality, and vigorously promoted.

There are other dysfunctional aspects of special libraries in public systems. Competitiveness among business firms, the proprietary value of information, and industrial security prevent any large-scale agreements among corporation libraries for cooperation. As a matter of fact, these factors may preclude even small-scale formal programs of interaction. Even when corporate librarians seek the open literature—journal articles and monographs—they must at times be somewhat circumspect, lest they reveal information of value about their work to their competitors through the chance association of ideas. It is not unknown for a corporate library to spread its requests for interlibrary loan and information among many libraries in order to conceal potentially useful correlations, even though all their material might well be available in one or a few libraries. Special libraries might well benefit from the services of more third-party agents who can help them use each other and the rest of the public sector, to map out search strategies, and to front for them in gathering sensitive information. These agencies might also be most effective mechanisms for tapping special libraries for the public, by extracting materials from busy industrial and corporate offices which cannot accommodate direct public access.

I am not at all certain that any regions with access to strong library resources in what I call the open sector would gain much by arranging to include corporate libraries in systems for cooperative sharing of resources on behalf of the public. Most corporate libraries are small and though they may develop subject collections in great depth, they are in essence duplicates of parts of the university and many public libraries that form the backup for public service in cooperative programs already. Perhaps some regions could obtain value from using material in these collections as added copies in case of great demand. But the geographical dispersion of the many corporate libraries that exist in various regions suggests that the logistics of getting these materials to the public would be most costly and difficult. This may be a situation where facsimile transfer of text would have significant application, but I am not too optimistic about the prospects of being able to design a facsimile communication system, given the almost complete lack of files of material in libraries in a format ready to be scanned by facsimile transmitters.

As a matter of fact, though, I would say we would be remiss if plans to improve the quality of library resources and services on a regional basis did not make every possible attempt to encompass the unique and the exceptional holdings of special libraries and the information retrieval capabilities of special librarians—at least for reasonable use by qualified people. Let me remind you, however, that collections of special libraries are very carefully tailored to suit highly specific goals for usually well-defined and delimited kinds or groups of people. To a large extent special libraries contain what would best be termed research materials. In size and content these collections are not suited to serve general public use by any and all comers. Thoughtful planners should be able to find ways of feeding certain kinds of data and information from special libraries into public reference service networks.

One of our greatest needs, if we are to learn how to use small, special libraries, is a better technique than is now used to describe and evaluate collections of library materials. We do not have universally understood and easy-to-apply standards or even criteria for grading depths of collections. It is difficult for compilers of collections inventories to interfile subject analyses of the many libraries involved because of the variations in subject terminology and depth of analysis: it is too costly for the libraries to redescribe their collections according to one standard subject classification. Proponents of centralized processing involving computers pose the automatic creation of a union catalog as an advantage. While union catalogs allow us to locate specific titles, they do not lead us to subject strengths in response to generalized requests for such guidance.

Systems planners are reluctant, also, to incorporate too much reliance on these special libraries because their viability cannot be guaranteed. Whereas academic and public libraries seldom, if ever, shut down, scale-down their level of effort, move out of the area, or change drastically the scope of their collections, this is not unusual in industry. Even the largest and most stable corporations have made such major changes as a result of administrative decisions that cannot be made to accommodate the influences of the public need for social resources such as libraries.

The efficiency of interlibrary cooperation is reduced by incompatabilities in operational characteristics attributable to conflicts in missions of the libraries of various types. Different kinds and sizes of collections and staffs, and different basic assumptions about the kinds of services that should be offered occur among academic, institutional, research, corporate and public libraries. The industrial library is oriented towards information and the librarian towards extracting the information, while the academic library is oriented towards the literature and the guidance of users who must extract the information in it for themselves.

A large research library serves its purpose best when materials do not circulate and can thus be readily available for use: the small industrial library serves best when it puts documentation in the hands of users in their offices and laboratories. Thus, when the industrial librarian calls or contacts a large research library for loans of copies of material, or assistance in tracking down difficult bits of information, he is invited to come to the library to look at literature that does not circulate and to extract the information he needs himself. Whether or not he can do this is a function of travel time to the large collection. Some special libraries maintain staff at nearby large research libraries (e.g., Shell Development Corporation at the University of California and the Smithsonian Institution at the Library of Congress) but this practice is severely restrained by the lack of space in large libraries to accommodate extra staff. There are other conflicts due to variation in missions but these suffice to illustrate the point. The existence of different missions is seldom denied, but there is considerable misunderstanding when librarians and users meet at the interface between libraries of different types.

A number of generalized solutions suggest themselves. One is to provide a buffer—a third-party service between libraries of different types—to do the work that neither the corporate or the public and academic librarian has the time to do. Another is to increase the public resource by building an independent, public research library facility strictly for the purpose of interfacing specialized users. Still another is to build an overlay on the existing system—that is, to recognize that certain large public or quasi-public libraries are attractive to people who wish to make special use of them and to add sufficient people and resources to these libraries to allow them to take on an additional mission. This is cheaper than building the same kind of attractive library in duplicate from the ground up. It is the technique recommended for New York City in science.[26]

Management in corporate and institutional agencies has been largely passive in the midst of their agencies' information problems. The impetus, the work, and even the struggle to arrange financing for cooperative systems and networks serving the interests of special libraries has come from the librarian group. As with academic institutions, management in industry and business apparently views libraries as increasingly costly. As long as librarians cooperate voluntarily, serving each other for nothing, management feels little pressure to seek actively an even *more* expensive extension of library service, regardless of the potentially greater return for its money through expanded access to useful information.

There are exceptions, and they are worth noting. Several industrial agencies in the Dallas area have been active in leading efforts to improve the quality of graduate educational facilities in the area. Library service is prominent among these facilities, hence when the notion of the Industrial Information Service (IIS) arose, it was actively pursued. Subsequently, the enthusiasm and the ingenuity of the manager of the service has extended its popularity in industry to the point where at least thirty-six firms now support IIS, paying membership fees of up to $9,600 per year. In Houston, the Chamber of Commerce, Rice University, and several industrial organizations likewise actively sought solutions to the problems of gaining access to technical and business information. It was this effort that led finally to the formation of the Regional Information and Communication Exchange. Now fifteen business and industrial leaders serve on its advisory board. Nevertheless, there is a wide variation in "information mindedness" among the managements of firms. Library systems planners should place high priority on the tasks of gaining active support from corporate managers, and of involving them in the management of the systems.

The impetus given to the joining of several kinds of libraries into cooperative systems by the policies and programs of federal agencies is likely to grow
stronger. The National Agricultural Library is setting the foundations of a plan
for a network of agricultural libraries and information services that will involve a
mixture of academic, government, public and industrial organizations.[27] A
national information and document handling system for ecology has been proposed in Congress, and although insufficient support was marshalled to create it
in the recent session, the Senate Committee on Interior and Insular Affairs
continues to gather arguments and ideas to support the idea.[28] The National
Science Foundation is actively encouraging societies to develop national information programs in the disciplines they encompass. Nearly 15 percent of
Chemical Abstracts Service's budget this year is derived from government
sources. Information programs that will in essence produce all-encompassing
discipline-based knowledge networks are under consideration and development
in biology, the earth sciences, botany, engineering, mathematics, psychology and
the social sciences. The articulation of libraries as operators in these networks
designed to serve researchers in various settings, is an endemic characteristic of
the premises under which these national information systems are being formed.

In any event, reference and research libraries will inevitably be drawn into
joint use of resources and facilities by knowledge networks. These networks will
involve the use of highly expensive and sophisticated data bases and communication equipment. This will drive up the total costs of acquisition of information
and data to a point higher than many individual libraries will be able to afford.
Cooperation for access, or at least joint ownership of data bases and communication and searching facilities will be required.

The grid of communication systems that is developing is not a simple one.
It involves reference sources on magnetic tapes, national and somewhat closed-
circuit communication systems, and the ability to talk in highly technical terms
with information analysis centers. Reference services of the highest quality in
the future will require far more than shelves of books to which one can reach for
answers. The experience of the Industrial Information Service is clear evidence
of a new configuration of reference networks. Through its office, local libraries
may tie into a number of networks and information centers, such as the NASA
Technology Center at the University of New Mexico; the TEXTAN Network
funded by the State Technical Services Act in Texas; COSMIC—the Computer
Software Management and Information Center of NASA at the University of
Georgia; and the Regional Information and Communication Exchange at Rice
University in Houston.[29] We can predict—indeed we must plan—for more of
this.

It is obvious that a plurality of library agencies and libraries are going to
exist in the United States, and that a number of organizational patterns for
library systems, frequently with several kinds in one region, will have to exist in
order to gain full power from the contribution that can be made by both special
and the more public libraries. Because of the complexities and peculiarities of
any viable consumers' region, we are bound to have different solutions to
problems of library organization, operation and use. Our chief concern now
should be that we have insufficient understanding and knowledge of each local

community so as to find the best configuration of elements to make serviceable systems.

Fortunately after many years of quiescence, state library agencies are awakening to the problems and prospects of their helping improve reference and research library facilities and services, particularly in metropolitan areas. In the past, state libraries have all too readily acquiesced in situations where large city libraries ignore them, and have put their efforts into other territory. They derive support from these non-city areas, hence serve them. This "pattern of state library policy-making prevents the development of conditions necessary for consideration of intergovernmental metropolitan problems."[30] Monypenny recommended that the states should "take steps to provide greatly enriched reference and research services in the entire state. . . .linking. . .strong collections by interlibrary loan and reference systems."[31] This, it appears, is what we are up to.

## References

1. *The 3-R's Program: Meeting Industry's Information Needs.* Report to the Division of Library Development, New York State Library. Cambridge, Massachusetts, Arthur D. Little, Inc., 1967, p. 13.

2. Bedsole, Dan T. "A Library Survey of 117 Corporations," *Special Libraries,* 54:615-622, Dec. 1963.

3. Shank, Russell. *Regional Access to Scientific and Technical Information: A Program for Action in the New York Metropolitan Area.* New York, New York Metropolitan Reference and Research Library Agency, 1968, p. 72.

4. Budington, William S. "Interrelations Among Special Libraries," Paper presented at the Thirty-Third Annual Conference, Graduate Library School, University of Chicago, July 30, 1968.

5. *Act to Amend Public Health Service Act to Provide for Program of Grants to Assist in Meeting Need for Adequate Medical Library Services and Facilities.* Public Law 89-291, approved October 22, 1965.

6. "MEDLARS to Expand," *Medical Library Association Bulletin,* 55:105, Jan. 1967.

7. Ellin, Everett. *Report of the Museum Computer Network Project.* New York, Museum Computer Network, 1968.

8. *Act Relating to the National Museum of the Smithsonian Institution.* Public Law 89-674, Approved October 15, 1966.

9. Mason, Harold J. "Industrial Research and the Academic Library in the United States." Unpublished doctoral thesis, Columbia University, School of Library Service, 1966; *The 3-R's Program: Meeting Industry's Information Needs, op. cit.,* p. 12.

10. *Special Libraries of Greater New York.* 11th ed. New York, Special Libraries Association, New York Chapter, 1967.

11. *Associated Science Libraries of San Diego.* n.p., n.pub., 1966.

12. *Industrial Information Services: a Technical Information Center for North Texas.* Dallas, Industrial Information Services, n.d.

13. *Regional Information and Communication Exchange.* Houston, Fondren Library, Rice University, n.d.

14. *Initial Report on a Study to Plan Development and Implementation of a Connecticut Library Research Center.* Farmington, Connecticut, United Aircraft Corporate Systems Center, 1966.

15. Shank, Russell, *op. cit.*, pp. 91-94.

16. Meyerhoff, Erich. "Medical Library Center of New York: an Experiment in Cooperative Acquisition and Storage of Medical Library Materials," *Medical Library Association Bulletin,* 51, Part 1:501-506, October, 1963.

17. Pizer, Irwin H. "The State University of New York Computerized Biomedical Information Resource." Anglo-American Conference on the Mechanization of Library Services, 1966, Oxford. *Brasenose Conference on the Automation of Libraries Proceedings.* edited by John Harrison and Pete Laslett. London, Mansell, 1967. pp. 151-162.

18. Cruzat, Gwendolyn S. "Metropolitan Detroit's Network: Detroit Medical Library Group: Five Year Progress Report," *Medical Library Association Bulletin,* 56:285-291, July, 1968.

19. "Bylaws: The New York Metropolitan Reference and Research Library Agency," New York, New York Metropolitan Reference and Research Library Agency, n.d., p. 1.

20. "Regional Technical Report Center Established," *Scientific Information Notes,* 4:1-2, April-May, 1962.

21. United States Office of State Technical Services. *Annual Report, Fiscal Year 1967.* Washington, D.C., Government Printing Office, 1968, p. F-3.

22. Nicholson, Natalie N. "Service to Business and Industry," *Library Trends,* 10:488-502, April, 1962.

23. Muller, Robert. "Meeting the Library Needs of Industry," *Minutes of the 62nd Meeting, Association of Research Libraries,* July 13, 1963. Chicago, Association of Research Libraries, 1963. Appendix B, p. 14.

24. Lesher, Richard L. and Howick, George J. *Assessing Technology Transfer.* Washington, D.C., Government Printing Office, 1966, p. 8 (NASA SP-5067).

25. Shank, Russell. *op. cit.,* p. 80.

26. *Ibid.,* pp. 91-94.

27. Mohrhardt, Foster and Oliveri, Blanche. "A National Network of Biological-Agricultural Libraries," *Colleges Research Libraries,* 28:9-16, January, 1967.

28. *Joint House-Senate Colloquium to Discuss a National Policy for the Environment.* Hearing before the Committee on Interior and Insular Affairs of the United States Senate. Washington, D.C., Government Printing Office, 1968, pp. 110-111.

29. "Industrial Information Services," *Newsletter: Technology for Texas,* 1:5-7, July, 1968.

30. Monypenny, Phillip. *The Library Functions of the States: Commentary on the Survey of Library Functions of the States.* Chicago, ALA, 1966, p. 162.

31. *Ibid.,* p. 153.

Craig E. Lovitt
*Lt. Governor's Office*
*Springfield, Illinois*

# GETTING PEOPLE AND INSTITUTIONS TO COOPERATE IN THE LOCAL COMMUNITY

My task is to discuss briefly intergovernmental relations as they relate to libraries in Illinois. My job assignment is in the Illinois Office of Intergovernmental Cooperation. This agency is a relatively new venture for the state of Illinois and was originally established by Governor Kerner in 1965 and subsequently strengthened by Governor Shapiro.

Several other states have similar offices dealing with problems relating to intergovernmental relations; among them New Jersey, which has had an office of local government under varying titles since 1917; New York where the Office for Local Government was authorized by legislative act in 1959 as a staff function of the governor's office, and Rhode Island which in 1961 created the Division of Local and Metropolitan Government as a part of the state's Department of Administration. According to a recent report, forty-seven of the fifty states of the Union have established agencies for local or urban affairs. These states, along with some of the major cities of the country, are wading around in what is a rather swampy area, but until recent months most of the states had not even entered the swamp.

These new enterprises in the government field have come into being because of the growing complexity of government, and also in part by the emergence of direct dealings between the federal government and local governments, with the states being by-passed. Efforts at all levels to simplify and streamline the structure of federal, state, and local relations are the current vogue in government circles. The problems we face are dramatically demonstrated by the statistics of these relations: more than 400 authorities exist for federal grant programs, and at least 160 federal programs have been added since 1960.

More than 1,000 new federal development districts, areas and regions have been funded. Here in Illinois, with our relatively dense population and high production capacity, we live and work with about 160 separate federal grant programs administered by about twenty-one separate federal departments and agencies. These programs involve more than $700 million and represent the potential for thousands of projects in our counties and cities. They are related to the different levels of citizens' needs existing in our society.

The problems encountered in the proliferation of these programs are not entirely related to their content, value, or impact. The difficulty has been that they came too suddenly and in such numbers that it is virtually impossible merely to keep track of them.

A recent listing of informational sources on federal and state aid[1] included thirteen catalogs put out by the federal agencies, four published by organizations of public officials, nineteen compiled by states, and six issued by other groups or special service units. The federal catalogs total 1,127 pages, the state sources 973 pages, and all others 567 pages, for a grand (or should I say, grant) total of 2,767 pages. For 1967 the Maryland State Planning Department published a *Manual of Federal Aid Programs*[2] containing 332 pages with details on 223 individual grant and loan programs. This catalog was hardly out before a supplement of 176 pages had to be issued to outline information on eighty-three more programs passed by Congress.[2]

There is a great deal of duplication in these catalogs and handbooks, of course, and finding a program in a catalog is just a prelude of things to come. The next step is keeping track of the guidelines established for eligibility in connection with a given program or project. Anyone who has filled out an application for a federal project knows what I am talking about.

Illinois has recently gotten into the catalog business. We have not duplicated the information available on federal programs. Ours, which was produced by the Department of Business and Economic Development, is rather modest—it is only 442 pages long—and is designed to provide information on *state* programs to help individuals and communities meet their own goals for economic and social development.

It would be a hopeless task to try to summarize all of these state and federal programs, but we have two suggestions to make. The first is that someone on a library staff or library board be designated as coordinator for federal and state programs. A few libraries have already done this.

The second suggestion is that the coordinator become familiar with three of the catalogs mentioned. One is published by the Office of Economic Opportunity and is entitled *Catalog of Federal Assistance Programs*[3] The second is a relatively new catalog published by the University of Illinois and called *A Guide to Federal Programs for Illinois Communities*.[4] The third one is the catalog of state programs published by the Illinois Department of Business and Economic Development: *Illinois Catalog of Programs for Individual and Community Development*.[5] If it is not possible for you to have a coordinator for federal and state programs, then these three catalogs should be on the desk of the library's designated coordinator for federal and state programs.

Intergovernmental relationships in Illinois are complicated by the number of governmental bodies in our state. All of us are familiar with the long-standing complaints about the overlapping of taxing bodies in Illinois—cities, counties, school districts, sanitary districts, library districts, mosquito abatement districts—6,453 in all; Illinois has more units of government than any other state. Intergovernmental cooperation, therefore, holds special significance for us here in Illinois. Illinois, with 1,256, has more municipalities than any other state. With a total of 2,313, it has more special districts than any other state. Cook County, the second most populous county in the nation has 466 units of government—more than any other county in the United States. The Chicago Standard Metropolitan Statistical Area (SMSA) with 1,113, embraces more units of government than any other SMSA in the United States. Is it any wonder, then, that we in Illinois government are determined to make this cumbersome machine of government work more effectively and efficiently?

Since federal funds account for more than 25 percent of Illinois revenue, and because officials of state agencies receiving federal grants tend to deal directly with their federal counterparts, the Governor and his staff run the risk of being by-passed and of losing effective control of large sectors of state administration. With such a situation, the principle of executive budgeting may be impaired unless provisions are made for coordination by the Governor's office. His office is the only spot in state government where the over-all impact of federal aid on the structure and functioning of state and local government can be assessed and directed into proper channels.

The principal objective of the Office of which I am a part is to improve intergovernmental relations at all levels in Illinois. This includes federal, state, and local operations. Miracles are not in the making, because our office is only a three-man operation within the Governor's office. Thus far the operation of our office has followed general guidelines offered by the Governor and a pattern of programs resulting from our own creation.

There are several other organizations in Illinois which also deal with intergovernmental relations. The Illinois Municipal League is, of course, one of the most active in this field. The counties and townships also have their own statewide organizations. Our office cooperates with these groups and does not try to replace them or compete with them.

There are also several legislative commissions working in this area. These include the County Problems Commission, the Municipal Problems Commission, and the Commission on Intergovernmental Cooperation. These commissions carry on research and make recommendations for legislative and other actions designed to improve government performance.

Too often, I think, we assume that more dollars will solve all problems. There are many ways a state government can improve local governments and these are not confined to broadening the authority for local governments to raise the revenue necessary to meet the problems of growth. Please let me make it clear that our office does not exist to duplicate services already adequately performed by existing agencies.

At this point in the development of our office, I can offer the following categories as being descriptive of our operations:

First, we try to keep the Governor informed of the feelings and thinking of local governmental officials. We do this by attending meetings of various organizations at the regional, state and national levels. We advise the Governor on proposed legislation which may emerge from these meetings and consultations.

Second, we have a dual role as an advocate of the state in formal and informal meetings with local governmental officials and as an advocate of local governments in dealing with state officials. We sit in on cabinet meetings in Springfield, and this means essentially that local government has a spokesman at the highest level in state government.

Third, we serve as a liaison with colleges and universities throughout the state which have units or individuals studying intergovernmental relations and the problems of local government.

Fourth, we serve as a clearinghouse of information concerning common problems of local government. This function includes making available information concerning both state and federal programs and projects.

Fifth, we can try to mediate disputes between local government and a state department or agency.

Sixth—and most important from the standpoint of librarians—we assist local governments in their relationships with state and federal departments and agencies.

From this brief outline it should be clear that our office at present is basically a service operation. As time allows, we engage in other activities which would be more extensive if we had additional staff.

One such project is the collection of pertinent information about local governments. One of our staff members recently conducted a survey of communities of 5,000 or less. He asked the mayors of these communities to describe their problems. He plans to use this material in a series of "think" conferences designed to produce recommendations for improving small towns. We are also hoping to develop a program for training local government officials.

Now, we come to the question, what does all of this have to do with libraries and librarians? A great deal because if we are to bring Illinois libraries farther along the road of progress, then intergovernmental relations become a matter of critical importance. Significantly enough, a report issued earlier this year by the Division of Local and Regional Planning of the Department of Business and Economic Development was entitled *Public Library Development: An Overlooked Aspect of Community Development.*[6] This report pointedly mentions that although public libraries "represent an important asset to any community, . . .they are often overlooked in community planning and development programs or given only cursory attention."

Under the Illinois Constitution, the independent officers in the elected branch are relatively free of the Governor's control in many respects, particularly in relation to the state's central system of budgeting and accounting. Federal funds for education, for example, are channeled through an independent elected office, that of the State Superintendent of Public Instruction. Federal grants for libraries are routed through the Secretary of State's office. And, of course, the Secretary of State wields the primary responsibility at the state level for our libraries. This division of labor and responsibility, however, neither belies the need nor the opportunity for intergovernmental cooperation. Indeed, without it progress will probably be out of the question.

What form will the intergovernmental relations take in the library field? We all know the excellent start made in connection with the cooperation between Secretary of State Paul Powell and library associations, special study groups, and individual libraries.

We have come a long way in recent years from the statement made by the Chairman of the Illinois Library Development Committee in 1965 when he said, "Illinois is one of the most backward states in the union in public library development."[7] This is far from true today because of what has already been accomplished, and Powell has demonstrated his concern and support for continued improvement.

Beyond this cooperation at the highest level, however, I would like to make these suggestions as a minimum approach in this field:

1) Not the least important is continued good relations with the Illinois General Assembly. I assume that the hard work of the Joint Legislative Committee of the Illinois Library Association and the Illinois State Library will continue to be an important factor in further improving what are already excellent relations with the legislature. Personal visits by librarians, library trustees, and library staff to their local senator and state representatives could prove to be of great value. By taking advantage of the months when the legislature is adjourned those associated with the library can call them up, go to see them, or invite them over for a brief tour of their library.

2) Do not overlook your local congressman and the state's two senators. Federal funds for libraries in Illinois amounted to $8,197,694 in fiscal 1966, and we should encourage our legislators in Washington to continue to do all they can toward increasing federal assistance for our libraries. I particularly like Ruth Polson's admonition in the January 1967 issue of *Illinois Libraries*[8] to "think big" in connection with finances. There is no better place to think big in regard to money than in Washington, because the federal income tax is the best means yet devised for garnering tax dollars.

Thus far, federal projects for libraries have been quite modest in relation to national needs. It is relatively easy to obtain agreement that library services and facilities are essential for the educational, scientific, cultural, and even economic growth and well-being of our people, yet glaring deficiencies exist in this most important and vital resource.

In fiscal 1966, about $530 million was spent nation-wide for public library services and construction. But even the most conservative estimates conclude that about $1 billion in additional funds is needed for books, records, personnel, and other services just to meet minimum standards. Assistance is needed for state library institutional services. It has been pointed out repeatedly that library services for the handicapped falls short of any standard measure. Interlibrary cooperation cries out for financial help if we are to make the best use of our library capabilities. The United States Office of Education estimates provided to the National Advisory Commission on Libraries (NACL) indicated that $4.7 billion for a variety of library resources would begin to catch up the backlog of needs.

These needs have led to federal activity. First came the Library Services Act of 1956 to extend and develop library services in rural areas. The statute was broadened in 1964 to include all parts of the country, and a provision covering construction was added. Library components (Titles III and XI) also crept into the National Defense Education Act.

Since 1965, Congress has expressed a willingness to expand considerably the federal contribution to libraries under terms of the Elementary and Secondary Education Act of 1965 and the Higher Education Act of 1965. Congress has added support for interlibrary cooperation for the handicapped, specialized state library services, and library services in general. Refinements in the legislation were contained in the Library Services and Construction Act Amendments of 1967. These latest amendments corrected several inconsistencies in the statute: extended 100 percent federal funding through fiscal 1968 of the provision for interlibrary cooperation and specialized state library services and added authorization for acquisition as well as construction of library facilities. The Higher Education Amendments of 1968 will continue federal assistance for another three years toward library resources, training and research in librarianship, and cooperative cataloging by the Library of Congress. In the closing days of the 90th Congress, Congressman Fred Rooney of Pennsylvania introduced a bill to amend the Library Services and Construction Act to extend the benefits of the state institutional library services program to the staffs of state institutions.

All of this means, of course, that an increasing number of congressmen and senators are interested in libraries and that more and more federal involvement in financial support of libraries is likely, although not at a pace comparable to federal participation in other fields. It is sad to contemplate that we are probably spending about three times as many federal dollars on oceanography as we are on our libraries. Whose fault is this but ours? We can start to rectify this inequity by urging our congressmen and senators to support libraries by legislation. The National Advisory Commission on Libraries has, after all, recommended "that it be declared National Policy, enunciated by the President and enacted into law by the Congress, that the American people should be provided with library and informational services adequate to their needs, and that the federal government, in collaboration with state and local governments and private agencies, should exercise leadership in assuring the provision of such services."[9]    This leadership will not very likely be forthcoming, however, without leadership being exerted at the local level.

3) Libraries must compete *effectively* with other local taxing bodies for sufficient money to do an outstanding job. This means librarians must go beyond preparing careful budgets and making skillful presentations to appropriating bodies. They must go beyond what is usually thought of as eliciting local support for library services. They must cultivate the other taxing bodies in their areas. If this is done correctly and well, librarians may end up with some of these taxing bodies quietly lobbying on behalf of libraries even though they are in competition with them for the taxpayer's dollar.

Librarians and others responsible to the library must talk to the chairman of the board of supervisors, the mayor or city manager, the chairman of the sanitary district, or even the chairman and members of the mosquito abatement district. They must be aware that libraries are aware of their problems—that librarians are sympathetic to *their* problems and they must become familiar with the libraries' needs, hopes, dreams, and plans.

4) You may well learn from these other taxing bodies ways and means of "making your pitch" successful in approaching taxing units. There are no real secrets in this matter of wheedling tax money. It is simply that there may be approaches you have not thought of.

5) Money alone, however, is not the only approach to intergovernmental cooperation. Innovative ideas can go a long way toward making up for lack of money. I saw a brochure published recently by the National League of Cities with the title *101 Winning Ways to Better Municipal Public Relations*. The ideas relate basically to municipal affairs, but they make interesting and worthwhile reading in terms of alternate approaches to problems. One practical problem facing central libraires, I should think, is how to expand reasonably and continuously the services necessary to meet the needs of suburbia. Perhaps it is time for someone to compile "101 Winning Ways to Better Libraries Though Cooperation in the Local Community."

I would like to suggest that there is a great need for getting people and institutions to cooperate in the local community. Cooperation is essential. It has not failed; it has not really been tried. I can predict that a plan for public library development in Illinois will find rough going unless such cooperation is forthcoming.

A glaring example came to my attention recently. There should be, it seems to me, a line of communication between the local library and such organizations as the Illinois Agricultural Association (better known as the Farm Bureau). The IAA recently issued a study committee report on local government that makes no significant recommendations regarding libraries. If the library is to assume its proper place not only in the community, but also in the thinking of the residents of a community, then such oversights must be recognized and rectified. Every report issued that neglects or overlooks the importance of our library system in the scheme of things is a step backward.

Illinois is slowly arriving at a recognition that the time has come for the library to assume its proper place as an important educational and cultural center for the community. But the leaders in this field must accept the responsibility for moving libraries up the scale of priorities in our system of public services and needs.

Libraries and librarians have an excellent image. It is an image of service, of learning, of dedication. But it is not an image of activism. Action and movement, it seems to me, are necessary if libraries are to be improved. This will mean the addition of a new dimension to the traditional view of the librarian, particularly in smaller communities. It means, in the words of the NACL, that "our libraries can strive to become a vital positive force in the social and intellectual reconstruction of a broadening and changing society."[9]

The NACL has made several salient observations, not the least of which is that "libraries badly need support in establishing new means of intercommunication and cooperation."[10] As they move toward improvement, public, school, and academic libraries will, according to the NACL, "all be obligated to change many of their methods of work, their interrelationships, and some of their roles and objectives in the years ahead."[10]

In his Executive Order creating the NACL, President Johnson requested an appraisal of "the policies, programs, and practices of public agencies and private institutions and organizations, together with other factors, which have a bearing on the role and effective utilization of libraries."[11] The NACL responded by commenting that "many different kinds of information systems and working relationships among a variety of institutions [will be necessary] if we are to provide effective access to relevant information for our society."[12]

How, then, can we achieve the degree of cooperation required to assure a high level of library development in Illinois? I have the following suggestions:

1) The Illinois Library Association, in conjunction with the appropriate state officials and other interested agencies, should explore the possibility of establishing a Committee on Intergovernmental Cooperation at the state level. This committee could explore all avenues of inter-governmental relations in connection with libraries and make appropriate recommendations. If this is done, the ILA will be in the forefront among statewide organizations taking this step.

2) Too often community institutions and governmental units work separately, through separate channels. This independent action sometimes complicates matters for everybody.

In non-metropolitan areas, problems resulting from the multitudinous existence of many organizations arise because of the difficulty of linking community agencies together. The lack of capacity in small communities is an additional complicating factor.

There is no ready answer to any of these problems because it is difficult to design machinery suitable for all types of organizations. Different things will work in different areas. But it is not impossible to establish a loosely-knit mechanism which can attempt to cope with some of the difficulties. I would like to recommend the creation of a Community Executive Board. This would follow the pattern developing since 1962 at a much higher and more sophisticated level through the creation by President Kennedy of Federal Executive Boards in most of the major cities of our country.

The Boards composed of federal executives in the major cities, were initially charged with the responsibilities for, 1) considering management problems and interdepartmental cooperation and, 2) seeking closer working relationships with state and local government officials with the objective of strengthening coordination on programs of mutual interest. The Boards have proven very successful in their own local metropolitan areas, and they hold great promise for the future. A summary of their operations is contained in a report published earlier this year by the U.S. Civil Service Commission under the title *Federal Executive Board: An Instrument of Progress.*[13]

My idea is that the community executive board should be established at the local level, either on a county or regional basis, with the membership made up of elected and appointed governmental officials, *including librarians*, who would meet regularly—preferably monthly—to discuss matters of common concern. As the group begins to generate a course of direction, members could also be recruited from important organizations in the county or region if they have a bearing upon the achievement of successful cooperation in the local community.

If I may paraphrase the mission of the federal government's Executive Board, the assignment for the community executive board should include the following: 1) to link local officials to new priorities of public policy (especially *libraries*); 2) to coordinate related programs at the local level; 3) to facilitate intergovernmental and community cooperation on programs of mutual interest; 4) to improve communications between local and state government and local and federal government, and among local governments. It seems to me that librarians and libraries should not shrink from being represented on any community executive board. Indeed, perhaps they should take the initiative in organizing such a group as an intial step at the local level toward creating support for a state plan for library services.

3) In major metropolitan areas or in locations where several different types of libraries are represented (university or institutional, as well as public and private), it might be worth while to explore the creation of a library executive board. This group should have a membership consisting of representatives from all school, public, private, institutional, university, and specialized libraries in a given city or region.

The principal objective of a library executive board should be coordination. Very practical problems would probably emerge as the item of initial concern. In areas, for example, where public libraries have been overburdened through demands placed upon them by high school, junior college, and college or university students, there is a crying need for coordination among public librarians, teachers, schools, principals, and college administrators—not to mention parents of students. Overloading will obviously continue unless coordination and joint problem-solving are forthcoming in the near future, whether through a library executive board or some other mechanism.

The same sort of approach to coordination would be helpful in alleviating the demands upon public libraries in metropolitan areas that do not correspond strictly to the jurisdictional area supposedly served by the library. Exceedingly complex are the complications arising in metropolitan areas which extend across state lines. I can foresee that once practical problems are considered and prove surmountable, then library executive boards would be tempted to branch out into other fields of concern, notably in the realm of library improvement.

4) A more specialized approach at the local level might employ the technique of creating a permanent task force on libraries. This undertaking should embrace all local organizations, individuals, and governmental officials who conceivably have any bearing at all on the well-being and future development of libraries. The task force would soon discover more than enough to do in connection with implementing a program for library improvement and innovation.

5) Citizen support is usually considered to be a key element in the success of any public undertaking. A series of "citizen conferences" might hold promise for promoting citizen support of local libraries on a broader base than that provided by the governing board. In Minnesota, the city of Austin and Mower County have recently engaged in a joint project of promoting citizen involve-

ment by holding meetings including citizens in discussions of three coordinated planning programs, as well as planning proposals for all of the villages in the county. The conferences are designed around ten discussion groups which are assigned the task of formulating proposals for making communities better places for living, working, and enjoying leisure. This citizens' approach has been described by the Minnesota Office of Local and Urban Affairs as "a unique effort to obtain citizen involvement in problem solving and goal development" and as "a new method to solve the local problem at the local level."[14]

John W. Macy, Jr., chairman of the U.S. Civil Service Commission, adequately summed up the magnitude of future involvement of local governments, institutions, and citizens in intergovernmental relationships. He also suggested an approach to problem solving. "We have little more than glimpsed the beginnings of the revolution in intergovernmental relationships that is ahead of us," he said. "Although grant-in-aid and other forms of intergovernmental dependency have become well established, . . .new programs. . .call even more for direct participation in national programs by local governments, and in some cases by local nongovernmental organizations. An equally, if not more striking difference is one of focus: the *problem* is the target, and all agencies that have something material to contribute to its solution must converge upon it."[15]

John W. Gardner, former Secretary of Health, Education, and Welfare, earlier this year underscored our nation's deep-felt need for cooperation and leadership. Our government, "with all its wealth and strength," he said, "cannot be fully effective without the help of vital local leadership, in and out of government."[16] The organization which he heads was created in response to these needs.

"I would emphasize the importance of the Coalition principle," Gardner said. "Some people think of the Coalition as just another organization tackling the tough urban problems of the day. But it isn't 'just another organization.' It is unique, and its uniqueness lies in the way it goes about tackling the problems. Our distinction is that we bring together leadership elements that do not normally collaborate in the solution of public problems—in fact, we bring together segments of American life that have often been utterly out of touch with one another—and, in many cities, are still out of touch."[16]

Gardner emphasized that "no one leadership segment can solve the problem alone. City Hall can't go it alone. The Business Community can't solve the city's problems singlehandedly. There must be collaboration among all significant elements that hold power or veto power within the community."[16] Gardner has summed up the magnitude of our problems at any level of cooperation by pointing out that "new forms of collaboration need to be devised even as existing relationships are re-examined." He has also made abundantly clear the necessity for involvement by all of us in seeking solutions. "Our society has become so complex, change so swift, and the social forces impinging on us so tumultuous that it's pretty close to being more than we can manage," he said. "If we are to retain any command at all over our own future, the ablest people we have in every field must give thought to the largest problems of the nation. . . . They don't have to be in government to do so. But they do have to come out of the trenches of their own specialty and look at the whole battlefield."[17]

If there is a hypothesis to my own suggestions here, it is that cooperation between people and institutions can contribute much toward creating a community awareness that libraries are essential, rather than marginal, to our way of life. Once this recognition is accomplished, the library will take its rightful place in the ranks of other community institutions. And the corollary to my hypothesis is that a policy of "creative librarianship" at all levels will point the way toward accomplishment of this long sought and long overdue objective.

We have a motto in our office which describes both our role and our function. We start on the assumption that "We do not want to know why something *cannot* be done *because,* but rather *how* it can be done *if.*" Our emphasis is on what can be accomplished if we follow the right procedures and work with the right people. We feel this is really what government is all about. And we feel this approach will assure success in the development of a state plan for library services in Illinois.

## References

1. Advisory Commission on Intergovernmental Relations. *Catalogs and Other Information Sources on Federal and State Aid Programs; A Selected Bibliography.* Washington, D.C., 1968.

2. Maryland State Planning Department. *Manual of Federal Aid Programs.* Baltimore, Maryland, 1967; and Maryland State Planning Department. *Manual of Federal Aid Programs.* Supplement 1, Baltimore, Maryland, 1967.

3. *Catalog of Federal Assistance Programs.* Office of Economic Opportunity, Executive Office of the President, Washington, D.C., June 1967.

4. Keyes, Scott. *A Guide to Federal Programs for Illinois Communities.* Bureau of Community Planning, Urbana, University of Illinois, 1967.

5. *Illinois Catalog of State Programs for Individual and Community Development.* Dept. of Business and Economic Development, Springfield, Ill., 1967.

6. Spear, Charles. *Public Library Development: An Overlooked Aspect of Community Development.* Division of Local and Regional Planning, Dept. of Business and Economic Development, State of Illinois, Springfield, Jan. 1968.

7. Trezza, Alphonse. "ILA Plan for Library Progress," *Illinois Libraries,* 47:155, Feb. 1965.

8. Polson, Ruth E. "When Your Library Joins a System, What Can You Expect?" *Illinois Libraries,* 49:36, Jan. 1967.

9. National Advisory Commission on Libraries. *Library Services for the Nation's Needs: Toward Fulfillment of a National Policy.* Reprinted in *Congressional Record,* Vol. 114, no. 173, p. E 9365, Oct. 21, 1968.

10. *Ibid,* p. E 9357.

11. Johnson, Lyndon B. Executive Order No. 11301, Washington, D.C., Sept. 2, 1966. In *Congressional Record,* Vol. 114, no. 173, p. E 9366, Oct. 21, 1968.

12. National Advisory Commission on Libraries, *op. cit.,* p. E 9358.

13. *Federal Executive Board: An Instrument of Progress.* United States Civil Service Commission, Washington, D.C., 1968.

14. News report in *Local and Urban Newsletter,* 1:3, Nov. 1968. St. Paul, Minn., Minnesota Office of Local and Urban Affairs.

15. Macy, John W., Jr. "Intergovernmental Relationships in a Changing Society—That Durable and Delicate Balance." In *Congressional Record,* Vol. 114, no. 64, p. E 3063, April 18, 1968.

16. Gardner, John W. Remarks given at America's Democratic Legacy Award Dinner, Anti-Defamation League of B'nai B'rith, New York, May 5, 1968. In *Congressional Record,* Vol. 114, no. 84, p. H 3903, May 16, 1968.

17. Gardner, John W. Remarks at Silver Quill Award Dinner, Washington, D.C., Feb. 8, 1968. In *Congressional Record,* Vol. 114, no. 84, May 16, 1968.

# DISCUSSION

**James Andrews (Argonne National Laboratory):** Each group discussion leader is going to present the viewpoint of his group as a whole and we then want to let any one contribute in any way they wish, either by giving reasons for supporting one or more suggestions from the group leaders or by offering any type of account or suggestion, argument or rebuttal. The topics break down into three general groups. First, discussion of the organization that might be developed as the beginning of an increased program for cooperation among libraries within the state; second, the possible ways of funding; and third, special projects, some of which might logically come before an organization is decided upon and others after the organization is set up and part of the actual work is done.

In regard to funding, Miss McDonald has indicated that there could be as much as $40,000 in federal money available which would come, however, only to match money provided within the state. This matching money could be provided by any one of a number of means, but any money available is probably going to have to be competed for and the competition would be against other projects that might be just as worthy. The money could be spent in various ways: for meetings; to pay the salary of a coordinator, a director, or consultant; or it could be used to pay for a means of communication or publication. We will now hear from the groups in numerical order.

**Mary McDonald (Illinois State Library):** Group one included librarians in Jacksonville, Lincoln, Springfield, Decatur, Champaign and Charleston—the strip across the middle of the state. Our discussion adhered quite closely to the general pattern that Mr. Andrews outlined. As for organization, the initial comment when we brought up this matter was "Deliver us from more organizations; let us use what we have." There was also general agreement that two concurrent approaches should be taken—the local cooperative efforts and the statewide over-all approach.

Three statewide organizational points of view were expressed: a) Build from the local level on the public library system structure already in existence, and expand the research and reference top-level structure for planning and for service purposes; b) the Illinois Library Association (ILA) and the Illinois Chapter of Special Libraries Association (SLA) represent, or can represent, most Illinois libraries; therefore, these two groups should establish a joint committee which would include a representative of the State Library, and which would plan, direct and coordinate the cooperative programs for Illinois. c) The State Library should assume the responsibility for developing and implementing statewide cooperative programs for Illinois. The State Library Advisory Committee should recommend expansion of the present State Library orientation from the public library to include other sectors of the Illinois library community. If necessary, the Advisory Committee should recommend statutory changes to make this change in orientation possible.

As for budget, our group recommended that the 1969 fiscal year funds be used for further planning meetings and to hire a full-time, carefully chosen coordinator—this appointment, of course, would require continuing expenditure beyond fiscal 1969. Any remaining funds after these first two kinds of expenditure should be applied to some portion of the following projects. The group recognized that priorities on projects would have to be set by the governing body and that by their nature some of the projects would run beyond fiscal 1969. Some of these suggested projects are strictly on the local level and probably could be developed without extensive expenditures of Title III funds.

As for the locally oriented projects, they might include the following:

1) Area-wide and eventually some sort of state-wide consolidation of film collections and services, eliminating by consolidation the small uneconomic collections that seem to be proliferating around the state.

2) Workshops for in-service training and development of further ideas, for small area cooperative projects.

3) Area book selection meetings, especially for the evaluation of juvenile books and then proceeding from there to more of a state-wide point of view.

4) A directory of the library resources of Illinois with location and the kind of materials held.

5) Adequate exchange of ideas and information; a newsletter on cooperative programs and projects should be issued as an insert to *Illinois Libraries.*

6) An accurate and complete mailing list of *all* libraries in Illinois, to be kept up-to-date.

7) For the information of systems considering the problem of unserved areas, a study to find out who uses the State Library, where these users are, for what they use it and how frequently.

8) Expanded high quality consultant services for all kinds of libraries.

9) Greater participation of the State Library Advisory Committee in the state's broad library picture.

10) Providing the coordinator with a plane and a pilot via contract with some company offering small plane service; a great deal of valuable staff time can be wasted in driving from one place to another.

11) Work through the Governor's office to encourage appreciation and implementation of the role of library service given by the code departments to institutions under their jurisdiction. This goes into the Title IV-A aspects of LSCA, and requires liaison with the Governor's commission on intergovernmental relations to develop its assistance in coordinating library programs at the local level.

12) Development of standards for librarianship, e.g., certification, salaries, and fringe benefits.

13) Consideration of library service to groups such as those under Title IV-A and B: the handicapped, and the inmates, patients, and residents of state institutions.

14) Cooperation in technical services—such as pooling requests for MARC cards in developing centralized processing.

**William Bryan (Peoria Public Library):** Our group covered the general area stretching from the quad-cities through Monmouth, Galesburg, Peoria and Bloomington. We began our discussion by talking about existing cooperative projects between types of libraries, and then quickly went into this same type of local cooperative project. Our recommendation is that local groups of librarians should start regular discussion on their own as soon as possible. They should involve their governing boards when they have something to tell them, and they should start cooperative programs as soon as they can. We observed the instruction to consider only next steps, and therefore, we did not draw up any details. In regard to the state-wide program approach, we felt that we do not need another survey but we still kept using the words "study," "survey," and so on. I think we meant that we wanted a plan for cooperation between types of libraries and we wanted supporting evidence to back the need for such a plan, but not just a regular thorough survey of everything in the state.

Our approach was to follow the program generally of the ILA Library Development Committee. We thought that the start should be made through a special committee of ILA, not the present Library Development Committee, but a special one that might even be a joint committee of ILA, SLA, CollegeLA and any other LA's that might want to take part. We did not believe it should be within the State Library at this point. Of course, we believed that the committee should apply for a Title III grant, through a contract with the State Library, as did the Library Development Committee, and that a one-year program for the development of a plan will be needed. There should be an outside paid director or coordinator, but here again we did not go beyond the first steps. We drew up a minimum budget of about $50,000. This was before I knew that more money than that might possibly be tapped. We believed that a salary for the coordinator should be such that it would attract an able person, one who could take a leave of absence from a permanent job perhaps, who would be paid enough to support two establishments for a year if he was not able to return to his home every night; if he was not from Illinois, he would have to be able to go home with some frequency and should be paid enough to do so. He would have to have a secretary and an office that would be at a convenient location for him, and therefore this means a paid office and not one provided free by some generous library or system. Our budget came out something like this: coordinator, $21,000; secretary, $7,000; office, $5,000; supplies, $2,000; travel, $10,000; telephone, $6,000. We did not attach a figure to meetings nor to printing a report and if those costs were added, the total would probably run over $50,000.

**Charles DeYoung (Bur Oak Regional Library):** Group three takes in the suburban western edge of Chicago, the southern suburban area to Kankakee, Joliet, Kankakee County, Will County, Grundy County, DuPage County, and parts of Cook County. We feel that as far as organization is concerned, some type of central director is definitely needed whether he be a coordinator or a consultant. It is also very important that a fair share of push come from the grass roots level, that the local approach is needed, and that not everything should be handed down from the top. We did not attempt to draw up a budget, but we definitely felt there would be need for planning, organizing, staffing, rent, secretarial help, expenses for group meetings, printing, publications and the like.

We had a fair amount of discussion about who or what group should get everything started; for example, if a meeting were held of representatives from various organizations, who would send out invitations? The feeling was that the State Library would possibly be the logical source, but it is swamped at the moment. We discussed various other sources, such as ILA and other state organizations, but we finally decided that the University of Illinois Graduate School of Library Science might be the best central source to start formation of an ad hoc group, inviting various existing groups to come to the initial meeting, by asking the president or head of each to appoint representatives.

Thus we propose that a meeting of this sort be sponsored by the University of Illinois, with invitations to go to the active state library organizations, including accredited library schools and any other agency or individual in the state who could make a contribution to the group, e.g., the Office of Public Instruction, the State Library, of course, the Illinois Audio-Visual Association and any other interested associations, and to ask the groups to identify the next steps needed to foster a state plan in library cooperation. We did not tie it down in any way; we left it quite broad in regard to possible activities or projects. We had the feeling that this should be left up to the thinking and discretion of this ad hoc group when it meets.

**Mary Howe (Lewis and Clark Library System):** We had in our group the directors of the Kaskaskia Library System, the Great River Library System, and the Lewis and Clark Library System, a private college librarian, two librarians from a public university, and a school librarian. We discussed how we could develop this plan with which we were charged, and we agreed that we should first align our services to the user and find out how we could orient these services to the user and that further, we should teach the user, that is, adults, youth, children, librarians, administrators, and so forth, where to get his services. There should be meetings with administrators and librarians of different types of libraries to iron out common problems, and other personnel should be brought in according to the problem to be solved.

By using the existing framework, that is, the already established eighteen library systems in Illinois, these meetings could be initiated by them and could be held either at system headquarters or the central public library within the system. Some of the areas of cooperation suggested by the group are:

1) National library week.

2) Career days or recruitment programs.

3) Resources, with specific descriptions of the subject areas available.

4) Making periodical holdings a part of the union list of serials of the twenty-nine Illinois colleges, as a continuing project.

5) Restudy and evaluation of the present network of public library systems.

6) A coordinator of interlibrary cooperation to be named to work from or with an ILA committee or the State Library.

7) Development of communications between different types of libraries; as a part of this point there should be an equipment inventory, a description of projects in progress could probably be a part of *Illinois Libraries* on a regular schedule, TWX should be established in the eighteen systems as well as the four research and reference centers, and a network of distribution of materials to libraries should be developed. This last point involves delivery of materials, and there is already a good start in this direction, including daily service between Champaign and Chicago, Edwardsville and Carbondale, and several other cities.

A directory of the libraries within the different systems is needed, showing the personnel, services, resources, and hours open (similar to the *American Library Directory*).

8) A study of the legal relationships between public and private schools and the public library.

9) Development of materials examination centers of both nonprint and print materials.

10) Processing of materials to be done by the most economical and best organization, and commercial firms to be used, if this seems best.

11) The problem of mass assignments made by teachers; we have all talked about this for many years, and there were some in our group who said that this problem should definitely be tackled and a solution found.

12) Automation should be considered as a technique to implement the interlibrary program. Every library, regardless of its type, should be encouraged to have a telephone.

We decided upon an $80,000 budget, distributed as follows: $35,000 for a coordinator plus a secretary and office help; printing and distributing the union list of serials, $5,000; meeting expenses, $5,000; and the teletype to encompass all of the eighteen centers plus the four R and R centers, $25,000. Finally, we felt that an editor should be hired for the continuence of the college list of serials if we were going to add other libraries to it, and that added another $10,000.

**Joanne Aufdenkamp (Librarian, Federal Reserve Bank of Chicago):** Most of the participants of group five were from Chicago, and I think we had a representative from every type of library. We have four formal proposals. One is that we need firmer knowledge than we now have of resouces in the state. We suggest that the College and Research Section of the Illinois Library Association and the University of Illinois Library Research Center jointly undertake a study of the existing directories of resources such as Lee Ash's *Subject Collections,* the *American Library Directory,* and the *Directory of Special Libraries and Information Centers,* to determine if this present record of resources is adequate. If it is not, they should make recommendations for obtaining the needed information. Secondly, what are likely to be the informational and intellectual resource needs of the people of Illinois for the next generation or two? Are the present institutions appropriate for their needs; if not, what ought to be done to satisfy them? The problem should be approached through a conference of selected creative minds, including librarians, sociologists, educators, etc. It is recommended that this be referred to the Illinois State Library Advisory Committee.

Our third proposal is to bring all existing library facilities and resources together in a unified state-wide information network. The present Illinois library systems' structure should be considered as a logical base to which all other elements of the library community can be added. This requires study of the existing barriers to cooperation and the potential demands which such consolidation will make on all units in such a state-wide plan. We recommend that the Library Development Committee of the ILA bring together the appropriate representatives of the library profession to begin this procedure. It is recommended that the present available Title III funds be allocated to the Library Development Committee for its use in implementing the development of the plan. And fourthly, in order to stimulate and encourage action programs in interlibrary cooperation as soon as possible, we recommend that the Library Development Committee of the Illinois Library Association encourage the State Library to create a position of coordinator or consultant for interlibrary cooperation to monitor and encourage activities, plans, and potentialities of interlibrary cooperation between all types of libraries.

**John Abbott (Southern Illinois University, Edwardsville):** I would like to reemphasize a point that Mrs. Howe made because I do not think it was otherwise brought out, and that is the need for a current reporting service. In most respects I think *Illinois Libraries* is very good, but it does not include adequate current information on projects throughout the state. For example, one project now in progress, the union list of serials of twenty-nine libraries, is not nearly as well known as it should be. Our discussion group was the only one to place any emphasis on the union list of serials, and this was due in large part to the fact that the other groups were not aware of the possibilities of this project. The editing of the union list is now nearing completion, and in my thinking we have the opportunity here for a broadly based list of serials. The University of Illinois list of periodicals includes something like 60,000 non-periodical serials titles; there is no national equivalent to this. *New Serials Titles* does not do the job in the same way, and it is essential here not only for Illinois but for inter-state progress.

**Father Jovian Lang (Quincy College):** Group three (Mr. DeYoung's group) proposed the possiblity of having an ad hoc committee meet and eventually from this might come a coordinator, as so many of the others have requested. During our sessions, my group discussed whether such a committee should be formed first or whether the coordinator should be appointed first and given the task of choosing from the various groups and associations the people with whom he would like to work. The consensus of our group was exactly the opposite to that of group three, because we felt that if a coordinator was appointed and knew what he was to accomplish, it would be much better for him to find those people with whom he could work. He could work more successfully with the particular men that he had in mind, whereas by having the committee appointed first, such an ad hoc group would get together, perhaps make suggestions and then the coordinator might feel that he would have to answer not only to that group but eventually, if he were appointed by some agency or authority, as would almost have to occur, he would have responsibilities in both directions.

**Mr. DeYoung:** If a coordinator is appointed first, who is going to select him? My thinking is that we should start the ad hoc group and take it from here.

**Father Lang:** We felt that the State Library is the palce where the responsibility would be, because the coordinator would somehow have to be responsible to it and no matter how we eventually work it out, the person in this job would have to answer to the state. Even if the ad hoc group were to decide on some person eventually, it is not going to be able to pay his salary and probably would not even be able to find him or to hire him. It would have to be an appointment by the state and this is the reason why we thought that working from the bottom would be less advisable than to have the person appointed by the State Librarian. The State Librarian would know what qualities this person should have, he would be able to call upon various people to offer suggestions as to who this person should be, and eventaully it would have to be his appointment.

**James Smith (Cicero Public Schools):** I do not think that we are at such extremes as it appears. One of the main reasons we went to the idea of the ad hoc group was that the State Library, as has been mentioned, is swamped, it is short six librarians, and right now it does not know which way to turn. In this case then we suggest that the ad hoc group be set up as a beginning or introduction to eliminate the confusion that we would have otherwise. The coordinator would probably go into the State Library, but the State Library at this time to our understanding is not ready to handle this task because of staff shortages.

**Mr. Abbott:** I take issue with that. I think the coordinator need not relate himself especially to the regular organization of the State Library. His job would be for a certain purpose, and he should not be called upon to do any other job. That is the point; he would be a full-time person for this purpose, and this purpose only.

**Mr. Smith:** Who would make the selection of the coordinator? We are going to have to have some local group to begin looking for a capable person—regardless of who his responsibility is to—before a program can be developed.

**Mr. Abbott:** It was our feeling primarily that should be the responsibility of the Deputy State Librarian, but we realize there is no Deputy State Librarian. We are assuming that he will soon be appointed and that he will give a high priority to filling this position.

**Mr. Bryan:** It seems to me we are talking about two different things and intermixing them—one, the drawing up or development of a project, and two, things that should be carried out within the project.

**Edward Strable (J. Walter Thompson and Company):** On the basis of the reports of the group discussion leaders, I think we probably would agree that there seems to be a tremendous amount of unanimity. At the present time we seem to be writing a job description, and it is not clear just where we are going at this point. Is it our purpose here to develop a broad program which will be passed along some way or other to many of the groups out there? Or are we in the process of working out the details of some of the main points that have been made? Are we supposed to have a consensus about the five points that we feel are most important, possibly with priorities given to one as most important followed by a second, by a third, etc.?

**Herbert Goldhor (University of Illinois Graduate School of Library Science):** Clearly from what has been said the implication is that it is the broad program we want. As one of the people who called this conference I can assure you that we do not tell anybody what to do. It is not for us to tell the State Library that it has to appoint a coordinator or to tell the ILA it has to appoint an ad hoc committee. However, we will certify all of these recommendations to all concerned parties. It occurs to me that there is no point in certifying to the

State Library only the recommendations that you suggest be implemented by the State Library. We will certify all the recommendations to the State Library and all of the recommendations to ILA, and hope that one or both of them will do something. I would agree with the implication that it is much more important for us to agree on a five-point program of what we think would be desirable to be done. It is not for us to decide who is going to do each thing and exactly when or how, unless we *want* to make some such recommendations.

**Robert McClarren (North Suburban Library System):** I would like to ask the five groups what attention they gave to the problem of definition of interlibrary cooperation. I did not detect it in any of the reports.

**Miss McDonald:** Group one did not go into this. The assumption was that it is any technique for working together among or between different kinds of libraries.

**Mr. Bryan:** It was our thought that it was fairly well defined by the speakers and that we did not further need to pick it up here in our discussion groups.

**Mr. McClarren:** I think we will be just as far along the route of cooperation ten years from now as we are right now, because if you look analytically at the premises that the various speakers used in their speeches you will see that there are three or four different interpretations of what interlibrary cooperation is. On the other hand we had one approach which viewed it really as an administrative problem. It was intralibrary cooperation and I refer specifically here to the presentation on Hawaii. Hawaii is an integrated administrative unit and the examples of the work being done there really represented internal problems. This was called interlibrary cooperation, but I would call it intralibrary cooperation. In our discussion group there was some indication that cooperation means that the smaller library gets the generosity of the larger, that the larger library cooperates with it by giving something. Although we sometimes permissively call this "sharing" library resources, in essence it is giving. There is a broader definition to which I would subscribe in which interlibrary cooperation is concentrated action for a common purpose without unduly or perceptibly interfering with the priorities of any one of the cooperating agencies. As it is for the common good, let us put the common good on a *quid pro quo* basis, but before we proceed with any planning we need to have some understanding, some agreement of what *we* mean by interlibrary cooperation; otherwise we assume the same goal but we find among the different presumably cooperating units that there is a considerable divergence or to what the goals are.

**Mr. Grable:** Group five spent about the first hour and fifteen minutes of our discussion trying to agree on what we meant by interlibrary cooperation. We decided to completely ignore the library aspect of interlibrary cooperation and to concentrate on its user aspects. I believe that our definition was: to provide complete intellectual and physical access to the library resources of the state for every user in regard to his work-related, recreation-related, and education-related needs.

**Orin Nolting (International City Managers Association and Special Consultant to American Library Association):** Since this meeting was called by the University of Illinois and not by an organization such as ILA, the University's

Library School staff has some responsibility, I think, of putting together the consensus of this meeting as reported by these five papers and by this discussion. After this I suppose the next step would be to go to ILA and the State Library, or maybe ILA first, and indicate to them that the consensus here is that somebody should pick up the ball at this point. The Library Development Committee is an ILA committee, and even though there is no Deputy State Librarian and the Library is short of staff, this is no reason for any delay. Dr. Goldhor can tell us what he plans to do after he puts together the whole story of what was said and done here.

**Mr. Goldhor:** As I indicated in response to Mr. Strable, we plan to send a summary of this last discussion period (rather than waiting a year for the proceedings to come out) to all of the appropriate agencies—and certainly to any of those named in the recommendations—with an invitation to do what they think they can to proceed. It seems to me that there are at least two main points that were mentioned sufficiently often that I take it the groups would all agree on. One is that there be some sort of a plan to involve potentially all types of libraries and all types of functions in a master organization. Just who would do it, how long it would take, and other specifics need to be spelled out. The availability of Title III funds makes it possible that it can be done. The second idea was that of coordinator to collect information on projects that are going now and to disseminate that inforamation to other libraries in the state, to encourage more such projects, to lead discussion groups or meetings on a local basis to get projects started that might contribute in the long run toward the state plan that will also be going forward—possibly simultaneously. Is there any third point that was mentioned sufficiently often to represent the general consensus?

**Father Lang:** I do not know if this would be a subsumed point or not, but most of the people I talked to during the conference felt that the single most specific, good new idea that perhaps has not been sufficiently bandied about in library circles is the fact that, as we deal with our public, we should think of the library and its functions in terms of the user rather than by type of library. Basically that would seem to be the primary objective of this conference, that we are trying to break down the lines between types of libraries and that the user-oriented approach was the single great idea that might in a sense revolutionize the entire approach to our services.

**Mr. McClarren:** In the group three discussions there was a suggestion which may be implicit in what has already been said about local activities: that perhaps some readily-identified and high-priority pilot projects might be funded and incorporated into this activity.

**Kathryn Gesterfield (Champaign Public Library, and chairman of ISL Title III Advisory Council):** It seems to me that this discussion has particular importance to the Title III LSCA subcommittee. In one of the first meetings we had we talked about the same sort of coordinator as has been suggested here but we never came to a conclusion. We also suggested a study of cooperation that already exists and the reasons why other cooperative ventures do not exist in Illinois; perhaps Mr. Wright has done this sufficiently for us now. We did not draw up guidelines but we did toss around the idea of possibly having some Title

III studies. I do think that a great many things are coming out of this discussion and the papers we heard here, and that the Title III subcommittee would now consider a study very carefully and make grants and some recommendations. I do not say that we should be the ad hoc committee that would suggest a coordinator but I do think that all of the new ideas that have come from this group need to be considered very carefully by this subcommittee.

Mrs. Howe: It does seem to me that what we have heard is that we do not want another organization started and that we should utilize the organizations that we already have. It has been suggested that the systems directors have been leaning over backward to demonstrate a true spirit of cooperation among libraries and in the light of what the users want. In our group, and now I am speaking for our group, we thought to use these systems as they are already organized, right down to calling meetings. Even if they could get only two or three people together at first, by adding gradually to the number they could get interlibrary cooperation off the ground.

Mr. Goldhor: It seems to me that if we are going to have cooperation between libraries of the same type, let alone between different types at the local level, we need to have some sort of structure, some sort of mechanism, some way of doing it instead of by a chance occasion when they happen to get together. I was pondering how this could be built in and whether money could be offered. It can not be legislated, you can make people get together in the same room but you can not make them cooperate. A possible solution may be to have the regional public library directors charged with the responsibility for bringing together the librarians of academic, special, school, and member and non-member public libraries alike, because this sort of cooperation can go forward independently of what goes on within the regional system. They might be able at least to make a beginning. In this connection too, I would like to tell you of an experiment we hope to start in the Lincoln Trails Regional System. The State Library gave the Library School its Title III allotment last year for "planning services" which we agreed could cover almost anything. One of the things it covers is this conference; we are paying for it out of the Title III allotment. A second thing we are going to do with it is to offer the Lincoln Trails Regional Library $10,000 to hire a librarian for a year and pay his travel expenses and salary to serve as a coordinator of relations with all other types of libraries in eight, typically rural counties. This sort of thing has been done in urban areas such as New York, specifically to promote relations between schools and public libraries; but this proposed project would be not only for schools but academic and special as well as public libraries. As far as we are concerned we do not care if this person gets the academic and special libraries working together, not even involving the public library. The only thing we are asking for our $10,000 is some hard data. We want some figures. We want the librarian to keep some records for us as to what the situation was before the project began and what happened as a result. It is only a one-year effort; if it works astonishingly well, maybe the System can support it or they can apply for a grant to continue it.

Mr. McClarren: There needs to be an immediate examination of the legal authority for systems to perform activities of this kind which are beyond the plans of service of the individual systems and the authority behind the plans of service of the individual systems which have the force of law, that is the rules and regulations of the state. I know in our particular case there are some activities which are wholly within public library administrative sphere of responsibilities, for which the North Suburban Library System has been censored by the State Library because these activities were not in its specific plan of service, even though the service was something which I consider an administrative responsibility in discharging our obligation to our member libraries. Even though it was very clearly in the public library area, it became a matter of determination as to whether the responsibility rested at the state level or at the local level. Now here we are outside the public library domain specifically, and in order to protect the systems and to authorize them to proceed there needs to be concern given and hopefully some assurance that this is at least mandated in the sense that there is authority in law.

**George Curtis (River Bend Library System)**: I want to second that point, because mainly the things we are doing with other types of libraries is to simply get the strength that is available in these other libraries; we had to do it, it took no genius to figure it out. It was suggested to us not to ask questions or get legal advice as to whether we could or not, which we proceeded not to do. We simply are doing it. I suppose there are certain dangers in it, but we will worry about that when the time comes. I do think there ought to be some kind of a broadening of the legal permissiveness of the program to be undertaken by the system.

**Miss McDonald**: The third recommendation of group one was that the State Library assume some new responsibilities, that the State Library Advisory Committee should recommend expansion of the present State Library orientation from the public library to include other sectors of the library community. If necessary, the Advisory Committee should recommend statutory changes to make this possible.

**Mr. Goldhor**: I thought the thrust of that was to expand the State Library's scope.

**Miss McDonald**: Yes, but this would be necessary because the systems are children of the State Library.

**Seymour Schneider (Northeastern Illinois State College)**: Speaking for an academic area I think that we ought to find out what we are able to get ourselves involved in, because in some cases we are not able to do things. I do not know about the other schools but we have certain limitations we must observe.

**Mrs. Howe**: I can not see how there is going to be any legal restriction on whether you meet with these people and simply talk. I do not think I emphasized enough that the administrator should be there, e.g., your superintendent of schools, because there is going to be some decision making and maybe he knows some of the answers that we do not know.

**Mr. Goldhor**: Yes, as I understand it, the idea is that the directors of the regional public library systems should have the responsibility for *calling* these people together, but it is not for them then to tell Northeastern Illinois State College that it has to open its collections to any high school student.

**Mr. Schneider**: I am thinking of financial considerations. But certainly we can meet and talk, there is no objection to that.

**Marie E. Woodruff (Jacksonville State Hospital):** I would like to take one exception with you; you said that cooperation can not be legislated. I think that the spirit of cooperation cannot be legislated but legislation can be passed that prevents cooperation, thus the school systems are prevented legally from sharing their resources, such as a film collection.

**Father Lang:** Along this same line, in answer to Mr. McClarren, the problem of getting all to work together is a big one. There might have to be a special relationship for private colleges, if they were to come into a system of this sort. I would think that the majority of private colleges, unless they are extremely young, would have sufficient materials of their own that are different which would enhance the collections of Illinois libraries, so that those who would be needing to do research in certain areas would benefit by the fact that the private library is also in the system. But if you are going to fix a very specific *quid pro quo,* it might be that the small college library would receive more than it would give. We have loaned books in English for instance to St. Louis University graduates because the St. Louis University Library does not have them. We have special collections in three or four fields which I know do not exist elsewhere in the state of Illinois, so that colleges as old as we are would have much to contribute. If there would be any legal barriers, they could easily be broken down because our administartion would certainly see that we have things to give to the other people and that we would certainly be receiving help from the systematized library service that would be given.

**Alice E. McKinley (DuPage Library System):** I think it has been implicit in what several people have said about this need for the systems to take some leadership and about the need for legislation for that, but I would like to reemphasize also the need for proper funding of any kind of action which would need to be taken because I am sure that the system budgets for the most part are stretched as far as they can go.

**Mr. Goldhor:** I do not think there is any implication that the system would necessarily pay for any of these things. It is just that the system director is the one logical person who would have general responsibility for this sort of thing.

**Miss McKinley:** He is limited as far as staff is concerned. It takes time and staff to do this, and it is a matter of paying for cooperation in that sense. There must be consideration, as in New York State, not only to the system but also funding from the college library's point of view; this is a very large funding program.

**Robert Carter (Lincoln Trails Regional Library):** I think there is no question that the broad purposes of the present public library system program, as stated in the law, include working toward the improvement of library service for all types of users, quite ignoring the organizational setup. There is the additional fact that the systems are the only existent regional type of library organizations we have in the state now to work with. These two things might be the justification for the systems taking any lead at all. I hope no one will get the feeling that we do not recognize the importance and interest and needs of academic and school librarians. On my own part I feel some hesitation at the thought that I should take any particular responsibility over and above these other people; I think we have to be careful not to arouse feelings of jealousy or sensitivity on the part of people from these other types of libraries. The legalistic kind of problem, about plans of service of library systems, really is just a symptom of the kind of basic problem we have in the present pattern of administration of the public library systems in Illinois. Hopefully this will eventaully pass away, and I do not think it is a barrier that we cannot get around, if we concentrate first of all on this broad responsibility of the systems provided in the law to work toward improvement of all types of library service and for all types of users. Within my own area, there has already been a kind of grass roots suggestion that the librarians themselves (including all types of libraries in the area) form an organization, and I am sure we will try to do it.

**Carolyn Crawford (Hawaii State Department of Education):** I would like to add a postscript to my paper. In reference to Mr. McClarren's comment about "intra" departmental cooperation rather than "inter." We were speaking of school and public library cooperation, but in Hawaii we have many libraries within the cooperative system which are not under the jurisdiction of the state librarian. We are at the point now where we are evaluating our ideas after four or five years, and we have discovered that it is our special libraries that are feeling the pinch—this is something you may want to think about. They work with a very special group of patrons, and in many cases they have only materials of certain kinds in the Islands. It makes a very heavy load for them, since often they do not have as much staff as the public libraries in proportion to the load.

Let me give you some advice based on our experience: 1) do not make plans which are too grandiose, and think of them step by step; 2) accentuate the positive in any communications that may go out, because the negative gets plenty of publicity anyway; and 3), when you start, try to find a common goal. We have been talking about this in the conference, and to me it is the key point.

**Mr. Goldhor:** Let's go back to the group one's recommendation about the expansion of the interest of the State Library to other types of libraries. I see no barrier with regard to academic and special libraries, but I do not see how we can ask the legislature to say that the State Library should have an interest in school libraries when the Office of the Superintendent of Public Instruction is specifically charged with responsibility for school libraries. Did the group consider that?

**Miss McDonald:** We did talk about it, yes. I think we should note that in our present enabling act it says that the State Library is responsible for consultant service to the schools. There is another law that puts this also in the Office of the Superintendent of Public Instruction. Because of the two laws we have been phasing out our service to the schools on the assumption that since the implementation of Title II (ESEA) is vested in Mr. Page's office, it is better for the entire function to be there. We can probably take the responsibility for school libraries out of our enabling act, but still word the enabling act so that we can work with the office of another elected official. I do not think that that should be too much of a barrier. I think that probably we would want to have the State Library enabling act changed, and this was part of our group's recommendation. Not that that State Library has not always been interested—we have always tried to keep up with what is going on in all these fields, but obviously we have had to concentrate on the public library.

**Mr. Goldhor**: One of your recommendations was for a study of who uses the State Library. I do not understand the reason for that.

**Miss McDonald**: I was trying to interpret some of our lending policies as a side aspect of our discussion, and some of the people in the group felt that this matter of unserved areas has implications for interlibrary cooperation. Since the system directors are turning their attention to this, someone suggested that it might be useful for the system directors to know about these people from unserved areas, what proportion of our work goes to serving unserved areas. Probably the better we do our job in lending books to people who live in rural areas, the less likely they are to be willing to tax themselves to provide their own service locally and consequently go into a system.

**Mr. Bryan**: There is another point here that has just occured to me. Now that the constitutional convention has been approved, I think we need to keep in mind that the State Library exists only by law: there is no mention of it in the present constitution. In view of the confusion resulting from the fact that there is a responsibility for school library service in the Office of the Superintendent of Public Instruction, and also by the law in the State Library, I think it behooves us, if there is a new constitution to be written, to try and cover this point.

**Miss McDonald**: The recommendation of the COSGI commission report on state government in Illinois that the Superintendent of Public Instruction should be an appointed official and that various functions including the State Library and the State historical library should be transferred to his Office has met with very mixed emotions.

**Mr. Stoffel**: One of the reasons for the mixed reactions to the proposal is that the Commission wanted to carry out the transferal of functions before the position of Superintendent of Public Instruction was made appointive.

**Miss McDonald**: The COSGI commission did not make this recommendation; a law was introduced in the past session to carry this out without making it an appointed office.

**Mr. Goldhor**: I suggest that after we get interlibrary cooperation established throughout Illinois we then tackle the question of the proper place of the State Library in Illinois state government.

I would like to go on with a brief report on the rest of the Title III money we are spending. I have mentioned two projects so far: the grant to the Lincoln Trails Regional Library and this conference. There are two other projects. One is a bibliography that Mr. Rike (from the Library Research Center) is preparing, on recorded experience all through the country with regard to cooperation between libraries of different types within the last twenty-five years. It is a very difficult matter to locate these reports since not many instances are written up in the literature or indexed. But we are getting some and perhaps we will put out a preliminary edition to get other people to write us of projects we have missed. Then we will put out supplements or a revised edition. This is the sort of thing that needs be done only once for the country, since there is no point in anyone else doing the same thing for the period of time we cover. It would be exhaustively indexed by type of library and by type of function that is involved in the cooperative process. We will just report what we find; if any two libraries of different types want to consider going together and sharing reference services for example, they can identify who has tried it before and by reading the reports find out whether it worked well or not and what the problems were.

The fourth project is a study in Decatur of library resources in four types of libraries. They have some good special libraries, particularly the one at the Staley Manufacturing Company. Then there is the Millikan University Library and the Decatur Public Library and the high school libraries. We will study their collections on a sampling basis, reference books probably, and periodicals and maybe notable books and so on, to see to what extent these different libraries have duplicated each other. Duplication is not bad necessarily, but if everybody is binding *Life* and nobody is binding *Look* it may be a result of each library going its separate way. We then plan to present to the librarians there a couple of propositions. For example, one is that we will pay each library a set fee, maybe $.50 or a $1.00 for each book loaned to the patrons of any other local library, for six months or a year, on condition that they keep records for us. Our hope would be that at the end of the year we would be able to show that they are lending no more books to the patrons of other libraries than their own patrons are getting from these other libraries. If we are wrong, if the Staley Manufacturing Company library is lending many books to the college and nobody from Staley ever borrows anything from the college library, then that is going to tell them what to do, and probably they will do it. This would all be written up in time—good, bad, or indifferent, and reported so that others might know what was found.

**Father Lang**: I was wondering why there was no specific mention of automation in relation to cooperation. Does this seem to be something so far in the future that there is no sense in considering it at this time; is it just that difficult to see how information can be gotten back and forth to different people as a phase of cooperation?

**Mr. Andrews**: I feel on that score that there might possibly have been a separate paper on automation but there is hardly a topic that was brought up for discussion here in which automation might not play a specific part—however, there is a lot of money involved in writing programs and getting them to operate. At the present time cooperation in sharing programs is excessively difficult because even though a program is written for an IBM 360 model 30, in many cases it can not be run on another computer of the same type because of different peripheral equipment that is available; one system may be set up for tape drives and somebody else might have discs.

**Mr. Goldhor**: The State Board of Higher Education is specifically looking into this with regard to the university libraries. A special committee on libraries has now been announced. Mr. Nolting, I wonder if you have any over-all view? Do you see any progress?

**Mr. Nolting**: I certainly do. Some of the material presented here has been a surprise to me and to all of us, such as the project you are undertaking in the study of resources in Decatur. I think these are all areas we need to study, and to learn from what other people are doing what we can apply to Illinois. I hope that Illinois will in less than three years come up with a state plan which can be submitted to the legislature as needed, but in many cases legislation will not be needed if you have authority to contract informally or on a written basis between libraries, as municipalities already do in Illinois, very extensively in the Chicago area. There is one thing mentioned by group one which is very important, and that is starting at the top. If you do not get cooperation from the mayor and the council and city manager, you do not get much cooperation between departments and agencies of the city government. It has to be structured to some extent, it has to have perhaps an ordinance, a contract or rules and regulations, and these have to come from the top. It has then to be carried out by the department heads and their staffs. We do not get anything done unless we start at the top to get it going, and then push and check-up and get feedback. And when you get on a state-wide basis in developing a state plan of cooperation between different types of libraries, this is of course a difficult thing; but once you get people together as you have here and you do not find any opposition; you may find difficulties but these can be overcome. You try to do what you can, not to start on too broad a basis, not to do too many things at once, as has been suggested, and perhaps to take the easiest first; if you get any one thing done, it usually leads to a lot of other things.